Data-Driven Decision-Making in Schools

Other Palgrave Pivot titles

Matthew Watson: Uneconomic Economics and the Crisis of the Model World

Michael Gray: Contemporary Debates in Holocaust Education

Teresa A. Fisher: Post-Show Discussions in New Play Development

Judith Baxter: Double-Voicing at Work: Power, Gender and Linguistic Expertise

Majid Yar: Crime, Deviance and Doping: Fallen Sports Stars, Autobiography and the Management of Stigma

Grace Ji-Sun Kim and Jenny Daggers: Reimagining with Christian Doctrines: Responding to Global Gender Injustices

L. H. Whelchel, Jr.: Sherman's March and the Emergence of the Independent Black Church Movement: From Atlanta to the Sea to Emancipation

G. Douglas Atkins: Swift, Joyce, and the Flight from Home: Quests of Transcendence and the Sin of Separation

David Beer: Punk Sociology

Owen Anderson: Reason and Faith in the Theology of Charles Hodge: American Common Sense Realism

Jenny Ruth Ritchie and Mere Skerrett: Early Childhood Education in Aotearoa New Zealand: History, Pedagogy, and Liberation

Pasquale Ferrara: Global Religions and International Relations: A Diplomatic Perspective

François Bouchetoux: Writing Anthropology: A Call for Uninhibited Methods

Robin M. Lauermann: Constituent Perceptions of Political Representation: How Citizens Evaluate Their Representatives

Erik Eriksen: The Normativity of the European Union

Jeffery Burds: Holocaust in Rovno: A Massacre in Ukraine, November 1941

Timothy Messer-Kruse: Tycoons, Scorchers, and Outlaws: The Class War That Shaped American Auto Racing

Ofelia García and Li Wei: Translanguaging: Language, Bilingualism and Education

Øyvind Eggen and Kjell Roland: Western Aid at a Crossroads: The End of Paternalism

Roberto Roccu: The Political Economy of the Egyptian Revolution: Mubarak, Economic Reforms and Failed Hegemony

Stephanie Stone Horton: Affective Disorder and the Writing Life: The Melancholic Muse

Barry Stocker: Kierkegaard on Politics

Michael J. Osborne: Multiple Interest Rate Analysis: Theory and Applications

Lauri Rapeli: The Conception of Citizen Knowledge in Democratic Theory

Michele Acuto and Simon Curtis: Reassembling International Theory: Assemblage Thinking and International Relations

Stephan Klingebiel: Development Cooperation: Challenges of the New Aid Architecture

Mia Moody-Ramirez and Jannette Dates: The Obamas and Mass Media: Race, Gender, Religion, and Politics

Kenneth Weisbrode: Old Diplomacy Revisited

Christopher Mitchell: Decentralization and Party Politics in the Dominican Republic

palgrave▶pivot

Data-Driven Decision-Making in Schools: Lessons from Trinidad

Jennifer Yamin-Ali

Lecturer, School of Education, University of the West Indies, Trinidad and Tobago

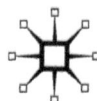

DATA-DRIVEN DECISION-MAKING IN SCHOOLS
Copyright © Jennifer Yamin-Ali, 2014.

All rights reserved.

First published in 2014 by
PALGRAVE MACMILLAN®
in the United States—a division of St. Martin's Press LLC,
175 Fifth Avenue, New York, NY 10010.

Where this book is distributed in the UK, Europe and the rest of the world, this is by Palgrave Macmillan, a division of Macmillan Publishers Limited, registered in England, company number 785998, of Houndmills, Basingstoke, Hampshire RG21 6XS.

Palgrave Macmillan is the global academic imprint of the above companies and has companies and representatives throughout the world.

Palgrave® and Macmillan® are registered trademarks in the United States, the United Kingdom, Europe and other countries.

ISBN: 978-1-137-41241-6 EPUB
ISBN: 978-1-137-41239-3 PDF
ISBN: 978-1-137-42910-0 Hardback

Library of Congress Cataloging-in-Publication Data is available from the Library of Congress.

A catalogue record for this book is available from the British Library.

First edition: 2014

www.palgrave.com/pivot

DOI: 10.1057/9781137412393

Contents

List of Illustrations	vi
Preface	viii
Acknowledgments	x
1 The Research Culture in Five Secondary Schools—A Case Study	1
2 The Challenge of Maintaining School Culture in a Traditional School Setting— A Case Study	28
3 A Study of Student Stress at the Senior Level at an All Girls Secondary School— A Case Study	56
4 Male Adolescents' Conceptions of Success, and Their Perceptions of Their School Experiences—A Case Study	83
5 Subject Selection at the Secondary School Level—A Case Study	103
6 Should We Re-Masculinize the Boys School? A Case Study	123
Index	147

List of Illustrations

Figures

1.1	Comparison of percentage of teachers in all five schools regarding use of data	12
1.2	Comparison of percentage of teachers who studied research methodology formally with those who know to analyze data to make decisions	14
3.1	Comparison of percentage of students with varying levels of stress	68
3.2	Conflicting experiences of home-related stress	69
3.3	Most common ways of coping with school-related stress	71
3.4	Most common student suggestions	73
3.5	Students' suggestions for easing stress at home	74
6.1	Students' ranking of the importance of certain qualities to their self-development	131
6.2	Number of students indicating which teachers helped to develop their qualities and skills	136

Tables

1.1	Response of research team to the project	18
1.2	School administrators' potential to foster DDDM in their schools	20
3.1	Students' suggestions	74
5.1	Number of students who did not get to do preferred subjects	109
5.2	Number of students who had to study subjects they would have preferred not to study	109
5.3	Reasons students gave for not liking subjects	110
5.4	Number of students who did not get to do preferred subjects	113
5.5	Number of students who had to study subjects they preferred not to	114

Preface

Are schools prepared for responsible decision-making through the use of data? Why should schools strive to become data-driven in their decision-making? If students are the future of a nation, are intuition and speculation sufficient to determine their future? The use of data to make decisions is new neither to the business nor to the education sector. However, both micro and macro policy-making in education have not shown evidence of the thorough and widespread use of such decision-making, either nationally, regionally, or internationally.

Data-Driven Decision-Making in Schools: Lessons from Trinidad captures the status of data-driven decision-making in some schools in Trinidad, a developing nation in the Caribbean. It presents case studies of five secondary schools which are considered to be prestigious. Each chapter reports on a separate case which represents a concern articulated by each school. The five concerns are

- the challenge of maintaining school culture in a traditional school setting;
- student stress at the Sixth Form level;
- male adolescents' conceptions of success and perceptions of their school experiences;
- subject selection at the secondary school level;
- re-masculinizing the boys school.

This book provides the stimulation for teachers and school administrators in any context to begin the process of research in their schools. It describes the process used to initiate the journey from articulation of the concern to collection of the data. Schools which are challenged by insufficient knowledge or skills in research will benefit from seeing how the collegial relationship between university faculty and school can be a constructive one. The role of the guide or facilitator, and the role of the teacher-as-researcher are evident in the elaboration of each study.

All five case studies include detailed findings under each of the five concerns outlined above. The chapters are useful not only for the research process, but for the issues explored—issues common to schools worldwide—perennial, recurring issues currently and in recent decades. The literature reviews presented in each case also immerse the reader in a deeper understanding of the issue as treated within the field of education internationally.

The book opens with a sixth case study which provides a realistic account of the experiences, knowledge, skills, and views of the teachers and administrators in all of the five schools in the context of the case studies. It provides a descriptive report of the research capability and potential for data-driven decision-making in these schools, using participants' voices and statistics from the data collected. Many practitioners in the field will be able to relate to the findings presented in this account.

Acknowledgments

I wish to thank the principals of the five schools who gave consent to and supported this research which was implemented in their schools. I also applaud the five teams who participated in the research effort as well as all the other participants in each school. The efforts of the unofficial team leaders, Mala Chin Fong, Darcelle Leanna Doodnath, Shelley Kalloo-Sammah, and Sandra Persad-Bassarath contributed in no small way to the successful completion of this project. I am also grateful to Rox-Anne Harripaulsingh and Vitra Ramcharan for their assistance with initial data analysis and general support.

1
The Research Culture in Five Secondary Schools—A Case Study

Abstract: *The purpose of this study was to examine the research culture among teachers and administrators in the five Presbyterian secondary schools in Trinidad. The participants were 130 teachers and 8 school administrators (principals and vice principals). Interviews and questionnaires generated data which were analyzed through simple descriptive statistics, and coding and categories. Findings revealed that many teachers in all schools would have liked to have been on a research team, and most felt that more research projects should be done in their schools. All five schools have the knowledge, skills, and willingness to conduct research that would enable them to make decisions for improved teaching and learning but for varying reasons did not do so.*

Yamin-Ali, Jennifer. *Data-Driven Decision-Making in Schools: Lessons from Trinidad.* New York: Palgrave Macmillan, 2014. DOI: 10.1057/9781137412393.0005.

Introduction and background

In the UK context, researchers from the National Foundation for Educational Research (NFER) were involved in a two-year research and development program with eight primary schools and seven secondary schools. This program began in 2003 and their focus was to investigate the research-engaged school in those contexts. Apart from the main report (Sharp, Eames, Sanders, & Tomlinson, 2005) the program team was able to develop a series of practical guides aimed at different audiences:

- research-informed professional practice (for teachers);
- leading a research-engaged school (for local authority advisers);
- supporting research-engaged schools (for researchers).

The NFER team identified the features that would ensure successful practice. These would mean that school administrators must:

- be prepared to commit resources to research—especially staff time;
- identify an appropriate topic and focus for research;
- form a research team and enable them to work collaboratively;
- provide support, including mentoring and research expertise;
- create a supportive learning culture throughout your school;
- make a commitment to embed research engagement in your school (NCSL, 2006: 6).

The reality of many schools internationally would reveal that research-informed professional practice is not the norm. As such, the findings of this research, though specifically contextualized to a cluster of schools in Trinidad, may likely be quite applicable to a large cross section of schools internationally.

The purpose of this study was to examine the research culture in five schools by determining their openness and readiness to use data to make decisions in their school settings.

The study is the culmination of a project conducted in five secondary schools in Trinidad and Tobago, a developing country in the Caribbean. De Lisle, Seecharan, and Ayodike. (2010) refer to the education system in Trinidad as "selective, stratified and segregated" and use the term "differentiated" to summarize these characteristics (p. 9). Alongside government secondary schools, there are denominational schools of which five are Presbyterian. The differentiation exists in that high achieving students tend to choose schools such as these as their school of first choice because they are considered to be prestigious due to their examination results primarily. The sample of schools selected was purposive based on those commonalities.

Data-driven decision-making has not been established as a common practice among schools in Trinidad and Tobago generally, nor are systems in place to facilitate its implementation in a formal way. As a matter of fact, initial teacher preparation for secondary school teachers is in-service and up to the time of this research, may occur at anytime along the continuum of a teacher's career. It is not yet compulsory except for promotion to mid-management and senior management positions.

As a teacher-educator engaged in the preparation of secondary school teachers, listening to their voices and observing their practice, this researcher has witnessed the tremendous insights that teachers' engagement with action research has brought to their learning and ultimately to their students' learning. The action research that they conduct during their initial teacher preparation is confined to their classrooms generally unless they are in the Educational Administration grouping. Research at the Master's and Ph.D. levels tends to be individualistic, driven by one individual. Therefore, the opportunity to engage these schools in a broader based collection and analysis of data was compelling.

Whereas tacit knowledge, intuition, and hunches based on experience may have their place, professionalism demands that schools be engaged in research if they are to use data to make decisions. In the context of Trinidad and Tobago (T&T), the extent to which teachers and administrators are capable of or willing to commit to this engagement is not known. This study is especially pertinent since it investigates the research "culture" of these five schools during and after the research effort. The research "culture" is characterized by the teachers' and administrators' actual research practice in their schools, their interest in school research, their research skills, their research potential, and their views on the usefulness of school data.

At this time, the T&T government's policy on data use for decision-making in schools is not evident. In its 2008–2009 progress report on its 2020 vision, the government of Trinidad and Tobago reported that the Ministry of Education "is actively pursuing the professional development of teachers and educators as it seeks to ensure that schools are staffed by professionally trained, certified personnel who will be utilising universally accepted teaching practices" (GORTT, 2009:73). However, the professional practice of teachers and administrators, and schools' active involvement in shaping policy have not been directly addressed by the bureaucratic policy-makers. Schools are therefore left on their own to initiate data-driven decision-making and where possible to use the human resources available to guide them in the process, as was the case with this project.

> Teachers engaging in *research* is the third seed of professional knowledge creation. In short, educational knowledge creation is likely to be at its most explicit and effective when schools are engaged in school-based teacher training and school-based research. (Hargreaves, 1998, p. 9; author's emphasis)

Data-driven and evidence-driven decision-making have gained momentum in the past decade though such practice was undoubtedly a theoretical construct long before then. The impetus to engage in school-based research initially resided in governmental policy calls for accountability and for justifications for claims worldwide.

Prior to Hargreaves's comment above, Butt, Raymond, McCue, and Yamagishi (1992, p. 51) felt that "the teachers' perspective [had] been missing from efforts at research, development, reform, curriculum implementation." In response to this claim, education has seen an increase in research by schools in an attempt to compete for resources, and more importantly, to improve teaching and learning in their own context (Altrichter, Posch & Somekh, 1993; Clandinin & Connelly, 1995; Goodson & Hargreaves, 1996; Roberts, 2002; Handscomb & MacBeath, 2003; March, Pane & Hamilton, 2006; Mandinach, Honey, Light & Brunner, 2008). Additionally, the concept of research use by schools is multi-dimensional. Much of the research in this area has been centered on achievement test results in order to make decisions to improve student success. However, Ohi (2008) raises the issue of the nature of the links that are present in the research–policy–praxis nexus. Is research-guided external policy handed down to teachers to guide their decision-making or are they encouraged to engage in their own research to drive their decision-making? To add to the research issue, are teachers analyzing their data appropriately and if so, are these data being applied in the best interest of all stakeholders? There continues to be a concern in the field that more careful attention has to be paid to the use of research findings. According to Bevan (2004:13) "research findings will continue to be filtered, fragmented and deployed to aid and abet practitioner fiddling." He feels that what motivates teachers is a desire to "extract and apply what is immediately useful to their daily experience and the challenges of the classroom" (pp. 12–13).

In their conceptual framework of data driven decision-making, Marsh et al. (2006) posit that multiple types of data may be used by schools: "*input* data, such as school expenditures or the demographics of the student population; *process* data, such as data on financial operations or the quality of instruction; *outcome* data, such as dropout rates or student test scores; and *satisfaction* data, such as opinions from teachers, students, parents, or the community" (pp. 4–5). Darling-Hammond and Ascher (1991) have also suggested a comprehensive system of indicators that may guide school administrators and teachers. With the wide range of indicators possible to point to data collection, Lashway (2001:1) suggests that we ask some questions: "Why is this information important? How much effort is required to track the data? How will we use this information when we get it?" In their discussion of data-driven decision-making, Marsh et al. (2006.) include the practical observation that data must be organized and analyzed on the basis of an understanding of the context in which it was collected. As opposed to clinical handling of data, they suggest the application of one's judgment be applied to the synthesis of data. They suggest two types of decision-making based on the data: decisions that entail using data to inform, identify, or clarify and those that entail using data to act. Apart from demographic data, school process data, and student learning data, Bernhardt (2003, 2004, 2005) also suggested perception data which describe what people think about the learning environment, and in her research she looked at the interaction between the different types of data.

As mentioned before, the notion of research-engaged schools is not a new one. In 1972, Elizabeth Wilson referred to Robert Shaefer's dream school (Robert Shaefer, *The School as a Center of Inquiry*, New York: Harper and Row, 1967) as one where "teachers can read, reflect, and design research" (p. 27). Such a school is seen to be both a producer and a dispenser of knowledge about teaching and learning. Stakeholder empowerment can be a major outcome of research within schools and by schools. Such empowerment can lead to micro policy making for the collaborative enhancement of student success. In a broader sense, it has the potential to inform and impact macro policy.

Teacher-as-researcher is a role that places the teacher in yet another role—that of teacher-as-leader. Such roles demand further operational necessities such as collaborative frameworks to ensure dialogue, sharing, and functional human resources and logistical systems such as workload planning and time-tabling. Such operational necessities point to the need for principal empowerment as highlighted by Gordon (2004). Principals as transformational leaders would need the leadership skills, personal characteristics, and relevant values in order to realize the type of thinking and action required of an effective research-engaged school.

School leaders stand to benefit from understanding and implementing the "competent system" as outlined by Zmuda, Kuklis, and Kline (2004). Such a system sees meaningful growth that focuses on change from the inside out as opposed to change that is imposed from the outside. It requires collegiality, information-driven reality, collective autonomy and collective accountability. Staff development is linked to an action plan which is tied to the core beliefs of a shared vision, and staff see themselves as a professional learning community (Zumba, 2004). A study by Shen et al. (2010) examined how 16 principals from Michigan, USA, used data to make decisions, and found that data do inform principals' decisions to a limited extent. Student achievement data were used to the largest extent, and mostly for accountability purposes, but different typologies of data were hardly combined for rich analysis. However, they concluded from their findings that principals will need continued assistance in adopting data-informed decision-making practices. Marsh et al. (2006) provide useful feedback regarding the factors that influence the use of data for decision-making. They report that the RAND studies help us to understand why some educators tend to use data more and with greater levels of sophistication than others. They had observed that some teachers were using data frequently to inform their practice, while others did not at all. They cited some reasons for the under-use of data-driven decision-making in some schools, including the findings of Coburn, Honig, and Stein (2005), which indicated that many districts without data systems lack the technical capacity to facilitate easy access to test scores. Access to qualitative data may be a problem due to gatekeepers' non-approval. Another reason educators may not opt to use data is because they question the validity. However, Marsh et al. (2006) found that high stakes tend to stimulate the use of data despite a real or perceived lack of quality. Both extrinsic and intrinsic motivation to use data were also seen as a reality in some school sites. They cite the findings of Coburn et al. (2006) which indicate that the lag time between receiving results of tests and the need for quick decision-making is also a factor that determines the use of data for making decisions. Another factor is staff capacity and support in terms of preparations and skills in formulating questions, selecting indicators, interpreting results, and developing solutions. This is supported by research conducted by Choppin (2002), Feldman and Tung (2001), Mason (2002), and Supovitz and Klein (2003) as cited in Marsh et al. (2006). Marsh et al. (2006) also reported the pressure to stay on pace with mandated curriculum and a perceived lack of flexibility to alter instruction as an obstacle to using data to inform their practice. They included lack of time to collect, analyze, synthesize, and interpret data as a reason for limited use of data. Even with help to analyze data, many lacked the time to act on the results. They have insufficient time to prepare for data collection, and even less to analyze them. They cite the work of Feldman and Tung (2001) and Ingram, Seashore Louis, and Schroeder (2004) to support their position that few organizations have been able to allocate and provide time for teachers to consistently examine and reflect on data. Organizational culture and leadership was yet another factor that influenced data use across districts. School leaders with knowledge and skills about data use and with a commitment to their use, as well as those with a philosophy of openness and collaboration were the ones with a strong vision for data use (Detert, Kopel, Mauriel, & Jenni, 2000; Mason, 2002; Lachat & Smith, 2005; Mieles & Foley, 2005) as cited in Marsh et al. (2006) as opposed to those who saw teaching as individualistic. The findings of Chen, Heritage, and Lee (2005), Holcomb (2001), Love (2004), and Symonds (2003) were also cited to support the notion that professional learning communities and a culture of collaboration do facilitate data-driven decision-making.

Methodology

This study examined the experiences, research knowledge, and capability of teachers and administrators within the context of a research project which was conducted in a cluster of five Presbyterian secondary schools in Trinidad (named P, Q, R, S, T for the purposes of this research). They all cater to students ranging from ages 11 to 19 approximately and offer up to the Caribbean Advanced Proficiency Examination level. In a meritocratic system of education, all five schools receive students from among those with the highest marks in the national entrance examination.

Though they are Presbyterian in origin and practice, their intake of students and teachers is multi-religious. Not all teachers have received initial professional development since it is not yet compulsory except for promotion purposes. Thus some will not be familiar with research methods.

A mixed method approach emerged as the most suitable for capturing participants' experiences, perceptions, and reported facts. Qualitative data were gathered in the form of a total of ten transcribed discussions with the five research teams, guided written reflections from them, and my own written reflections. This in-depth focus on these team members was crucial to gain an understanding of how teachers feel and think as they engage in research planning and implementing.

Closed-ended questionnaires administered to 130 teachers from the five schools, seven research team members, and eight school administrators generated quantitative data after the research intervention in the five schools. Because these persons formed the research context and determined the research culture of the schools, a large number of details needed to be captured in order to understand their readiness for using data to make decisions.

A phenomenon peculiar to this research context was that I was a "partial insider" in that I initiated the overall project in the five schools, worked alongside the research teams, co-planned the data collection with them and analyzed the data. The teams were instrumental in collecting the data for the project in their own schools. This study presents findings based on the experience of the projects in the five schools. For each school, I orally presented the findings of their research to the staff and administrators who could be present at the time. It was at that time that I administered the questionnaires for this study. "Partial insiderness" is also due to the fact that I am familiar to many of the staff members of all of the five schools through both professional and personal channels. Consequently, school participation was not as problematic as it could have been otherwise.

The following research questions guided this study:

1   What were the initial responses of the research teams and administrators to the concept of a research intervention in their school?
2   What were the non-researcher teachers' responses to the experience of a data-driven decision-making intervention in their context?

3   How do the teachers in general use school data?
4   To what extent are the teachers in general actually capable of conducting research?
5   To what extent do the teachers in general demonstrate the potential for conducting research?
6   What were the research teams' responses to the experience of a data-driven decision-making intervention in their context?
7   What is the potential of school administrators to foster data-driven decision-making in their schools?

Findings

Initial responses of the research teams and administrators to the concept of a research intervention in their school

Gaining entry: I had experienced no problems with gaining the support of the five principals to carry out this project in their schools. Each principal had agreed to identify a small team who would work with me on the project. Arranging teams and initial meetings became a challenge since issues of "very busy," "heavy workload" arose despite the words of one who said: "I felt that whatever area of data-driven decision-making research we chose to delve into, that it would be valuable to the school community, since the initiative seemed to be geared toward the improvement of systems, for the benefit of the student."

Time

"Time," "other commitments," "heavy time-table," "personal reasons," "unable to schedule appointment times that coincide with our spare time due to classes," "the teaching of new syllabi," and "additional extra-curricular responsibilities at school" were reasons cited by some teachers for not being able to participate in the research effort.

Interest/Enthusiasm/Willingness

In all schools I was encouraged by the interesting discussion that ensued, and participants were vocal about their enthusiasm for the research since examination of the topics was much needed in their school.

The points raised generally indicated analytic reflection. Their enthusiasm seemed to spring from the fact that the choice of research was from *their* perspective. "It was interesting that they were all passionate about a specific issue... I was pleasantly surprised by their enthusiasm and was hoping that it would not decrease as the process developed... I left feeling very uplifted by the attitude to the project."[1]

Deciding on a topic

At each school there were definite issues that the teachers suggested for their research. Some negotiation was required in all cases to narrow the focus down to one issue. My role was to clearly define the issue so that it represented the intention of the teachers.

Non-researcher teachers' responses to the experience of a data-driven decision-making intervention in their context

Responses to this research effort compared among the five schools

It was interesting to note that the percentage of teachers who were aware of a research team in their school ranged from 50% to 79%. This is perhaps an indication that the project was not initiated by the school but by an "outsider", even though the issues selected for investigation were suggested by the schools' teams. Another factor may have been that the teams tried not to be too intrusive on their colleagues' time since "lack of time" was reported to be a factor that prevented some teachers from conducting research.

Even fewer teachers than those who were aware of a research team on their staff claimed not to know which teachers comprised the research team. These percentages ranged from 47% to 54%. Strangely, the school with the smallest percentage of teachers who knew there was a research team working on a project was the one with the largest percentage of teachers who knew which teachers comprised the research team. In a parallel vein, although School R had the largest percentage of teachers who were aware of the existence of a research team, their staff had the smallest percentage of teachers who knew who the teachers actually were. This may have been due to the fact that midway in the project, the team in that school had dismantled due to workload constraints. Except for one school (P), not all the teachers who were aware of a research team in the school could identify who they were. Up to 32% of one teaching staff was vague about who were involved in this research project in their school.

Having seen that there were varying percentages of teachers who did not know that there was a research team in the school, it is logical that the percentage of teachers who were not interested in the research issue ranged from 13% to 44% with an average of 25% per school. An interesting phenomenon was that although School S had the highest percentage of teachers (76%) who said they were interested in the research issue, only 59% of them had filled out the questionnaire provided by the research team. The high interest may also indicate that the issue of subject selection is a burning one at the school.

Both School P and School T had relatively high percentages of teachers who would have liked to have been involved in the research project. These two schools showed the highest percentages of teachers who indicated that their school's administration encourages the use of data to make decisions.

Although when compared to the other four schools, School S had the largest percentage of teachers who were interested in the research issue (76%), only 47% indicated that they would have liked to have been involved in the project, with 12% indicating a "sort of" interest, making an overall total of 59% with some desire to have been involved.

Generally, the research did not appear to cause tension among staff except for School S where 21% felt it did cause tension and 29% felt it "sort of" caused tension, totaling 50% indicating some degree of tension. It had been noted earlier that this was the school where teachers indicated the most amount of interest in the issue researched. The lack of tension may also be linked to the fact that 50% to 79% of teachers in the schools were not aware of a research team in their school. One also recalls that an average of 25% per school had no interest in the issue researched in their own school.

Although significant percentages of teachers had no interest in the issue researched, or would not have liked to have been involved in the research, many more teachers felt that their school should do more research projects like this one. The highest percentage of teachers in any one school who felt that their school should not be involved in research projects like this was 13%, with the same percentage in the same school not being quite sure, having chosen the "sort of" option. This was the school where the team was dismantled before the end of the project due to time-tabling constraints.

12 Data-Driven Decision-Making in Schools

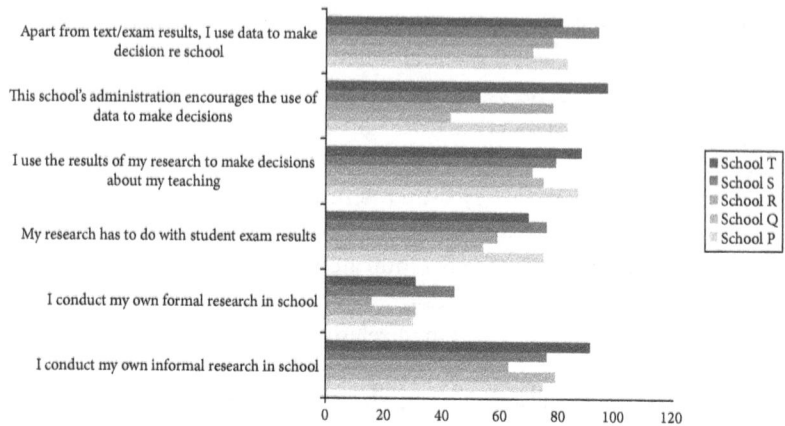

FIGURE 1.1 *Comparison of percentage of teachers in all five schools regarding use of data*

Teachers' use of data

Figure 1.1 provides data on the current research practice among teachers in these five schools, giving a sense of the potential for data-driven decision-making in these contexts. The area of least involvement for all schools was in conducting formal research. Yet, relatively large percentages indicated that they use results of their research to make decisions about their teaching. We may conclude that many of these teachers rely on hunches or tacit knowledge to inform their decisions. Even in the schools where there were high percentages of teachers who reported that their administration encouraged the use of data to make decisions, the percentages of teachers in those schools who conducted formal research were comparatively low.

Between 60% and 91% of the teachers report that they do conduct their own informal research in their schools. The school whose team was dismantled during the research was the one with the lowest percentage of teachers involved in both formal and informal research. This may be perceived as a trend in that school in terms of the research culture.

In terms of how they use data, in each of the schools, while an average of 67% said their research has to do with test/exam results, a larger percentage in each school (average of 81%) indicated that they used data other than test results.

The percentages of teachers who reported that their administration encourages the use of data to make decisions ranged from 43% to

97%. School T recorded the highest percentage (97%) and was also the one where the most teachers reported conducting informal research. Together with School P, which had a high percentage of teachers (83%) indicating that their administration encouraged the use of data to make decisions, School T demonstrated a high occurrence of teachers using data to make decisions.

Teachers' actual research capability

Most teachers in three of the five schools have studied research methodology, though relatively small percentages indicated that they had studied it insufficiently. In School R and School T, there were 35% to 37% who indicated that they hadn't studied it formally. This may indicate that these were the teachers who hadn't done their postgraduate diploma in education. Yet, among those who had indicated that they had done it, there were a few who said that they had not studied research methodology formally. This may require further investigation. In all schools there were varying percentages of teachers who felt they had studied it insufficiently. This is perhaps an indication that there is room for continuing professional development in this area for teachers in all five schools.

In these five schools the percentages of teachers with an understanding of how to conduct research formally vary from 50% to 79%. There is a general similarity in the percentages of teachers who studied research methodology formally and who understand how to conduct research formally. However, in two schools (School R and School T), the percentage of teachers who understand how to conduct research formally is larger than the percentage who actually said that they had studied it formally (in School R 42% studied it and 58% understand it, and in School T 35% studied it and 50% understand it). This phenomenon requires further investigation.

Regardless of teachers' research capability, the reality of collaborative work is a major factor in determining the extent to which meaningful and practical research can be carried out in a school by a school community. The percentages of teachers who felt that they could get colleagues to work collaboratively on research in school varied from 31% to 74%. The school with the highest percentage (School P) recorded a relatively high percentage of teachers who felt that their administration encouraged them to use data to make decisions. However, this research produces no evidence to indicate a relationship between administration's attitude to teacher research and the ability to engage in collaborative research in school.

School P emerges as the school where the highest percentage of teachers know how to factor research into their schedule. This supports the finding that more than 75% of them had indicated that they conduct research informally and use data to make decisions in addition to being encouraged by their administration to do so. The data may, but not necessarily, explain the problem of time which was raised by the five teams when the project was initiated. In four out of the five schools, there was evidence that between 43% and 59% of teachers either did not know or knew insufficiently how to find the time to conduct research. "Time" may have been a factor in the scheduling of research.

Figure 1.2 tells us that except for School S, in all the schools, more teachers felt they were able to analyze data for decision-making than those who studied research methodology formally. This is an indication that either they have learnt to analyze data from sources other than through formal channels, or that they are assuming that they know how to analyze data. It may be that through the act of doing it at school they have become familiar with some data analysis processes. It has been noted before that a fairly large percentage of the teachers use examination results as their data. However, it is not possible at this time to determine how the data are analyzed or for what purposes. The general disparity between formal study of methodology and knowing how to

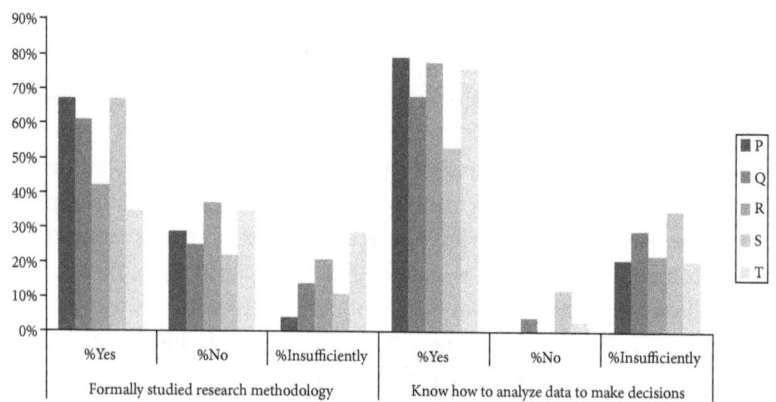

FIGURE 1.2 *Comparison of percentage of teachers who studied research methodology formally with those who know to analyze data to make decisions*

analyze seems to be an area for further research, especially with a view to pragmatic teacher development.

Between 69% and 89% of teachers in the five schools were aware that they could use existing data to better understand teaching and learning in their schools. Even though the percentages who did not know or who were not sure were small, it still points to a need for professional guidance in those contexts. The school with the most significant need in developing data awareness is School R, where 25% of the 20 teachers who responded to the questionnaire did not know that there is always data which they could analyze. However, 78% of them had indicated that they knew how to analyze data. There therefore seems to be a need to build the research awareness of some teachers in School R.

Teachers' potential research capability

A large percentage of teachers in each of the five schools would like to find out how to conduct research in their school in an efficient and practical way. The largest percentage of teachers who were not interested (22%) came from a school where they did not conduct research because of a lack of collegial support (95%) and a lack of support from school administration (63%). Almost all teachers would like school-based research to be a "buy in" from all staff and administration. It was not ascertained why there were small percentages of teachers who did not care for this "buy in".

Almost all teachers were able to identify areas in their school which research can help to improve, thus recognizing the potential usefulness of conducting research. In all five schools, all teachers deemed research to be a component of teacher professionalism except for one teacher who had not yet done initial teacher development. Most teachers were able to identify areas in their school which research can help to improve, with the exception of three teachers who had not done the standard local "Dip. Ed.". There was one teacher whose responses were contradictory in that she reported a general lack of interest in or support for school-based research, but felt that using research is a component of teacher professionalism.

The percentage of teachers among the five schools who found that time prevented them from conducting research ranged from 76% to 95%. However, lack of collegial support (average of 58%) and support from administration (average of 49%) were also reported to be obstacles for significant percentages of teachers. School P showed least evidence of the latter two obstacles to conducting research.

The idea of more professional development workshops was supported by most teachers while 79% to 100% of the teachers indicated that they would like to pursue further qualifications in education.

In conclusion, there is much potential for research output by teachers in these schools but there seems to be a deficit of support both by administration and colleagues. However, due to the fairly common concern about lack of time, it seems that administration has a role to play in motivating teachers as researchers and in facilitating the conduct and analysis of their research. Team building strategies also seem to be a necessary focus for all five schools.

Comparing the views of the five schools on the usefulness of this research project

In all five schools, teachers were of the opinion that this research project was useful for the development of their whole school and for their own teaching. Most were sure whereas a few felt that it "may be" useful in both ways. In one school, however, there were two teachers who felt that this research project had no use, and those two in addition to another were not motivated by the research results to conduct their own formal research at school.

Research teams' experience of the research project

Initial feelings about involvement in the project

As indicated in the opening section of this report, initial co-opting of teams in each school was a challenge in most cases. Although there was the fear of the time commitment that would be required of them, there were many positive feelings expressed initially by the teachers. These feelings, expressed by individual members of the teams, are detailed below.

Research skills

> Since my purpose for becoming involved was initially selfish (in that I needed to familiarise myself with researching a school problem...I immediately volunteered since I knew that I had my MEd thesis to do and I would have to do some research like this and I thought that this might help me put my thoughts into focus for that...I came away from the meeting with a clearer understanding of how to approach my thesis/ project.

I think that this project will help develop my research and analytic skills and also prepare me for further professional development e.g. Dip. Ed. so I am honoured to be a part of something that realistically seeks to understand/improve a student's experience of school.

Relevance to their school

From prior discussions with[colleague's name] and having had access to information about the number of students who did not want to do Spanish this year at Form 3, I have sensed that this is an area of concern and I was happy that this was being addressed.

I liked the fact that it catered to the needs of the school, teachers and students. I was pleased to know that a research case was not imposed on us, but rather we, the teachers, were given a chance to speak out about our concerns and try to correct the apparent problems.

Whole school improvement

The impact of the research, not just for a year group that we, the deans, are having some difficulty with, but also as it relates to the impact on the school and how the curriculum is shaped.

I felt that whatever area of data-driven decision-making research we chose to delve into, that it would be valuable to the school community, since the initiative seemed to be geared toward the improvement of systems, for the benefit of the student.

Sharing

...the prospect of sharing this research with our Presbyterian sister and brother schools, so that we can work in co-operation rather than competition.

After initial discussions, I felt that the research would be...very pertinent to the issues affecting teachers in all five Presbyterian Secondary Schools.

Excitement/Intrigue/Interest

The project seemed interesting...Initially I was intrigued by the research.

I became excited during the discussions as ideas began to flow about the impact of the research.

After initial discussions, I felt that the research would be exciting.

What they appreciated

I liked the atmosphere of openness. There was an atmosphere of co-operation even though there may have been some initial hesitation since some of the participants were initially "volunteered".

Upon sharing my concerns with [the project coordinator] I was reassured of the level of involvement expected "as a team." Needless to say, I no longer have my previous concerns.

I found [the project coordinator] to be professional, accommodating, understanding (especially when I had to leave early, changing meeting dates) knowledgeable and eager about her proposal.

How the teams responded after the project

Table 1.1 outlines varying responses of the teams to the research project in their own schools.

Since the topics for research were selected by each team, it is expected that they would have found the research to have had relevance to their own school. Out of the seven members, only four felt that they had participated sufficiently, while three felt they did to some extent and

TABLE 1.1   *Response of research team to the project*

	Overall no. of members of research teams (N7)		
	Yes	No	To Some Extent
The issue researched was of relevance to this school	7		
I participated sufficiently in this project	4	1	2
I wish I had more time in order to analyze the data myself	4	2	1
I tried to persuade colleagues on staff of the relevance of the research	3	2	2
This research sparked more staff discussion on the issue	3	1	3
This project caused tension on staff	2	3	2
The school should do more projects like this	4		2

one was sure that she did not. While four would have definitely liked to analyze the data, and one would have liked to do so to some extent, two of them would not have liked to analyze even with available time. It may be that these teachers did not have the research skills or this would have meant a heavier workload. Persuading colleagues of the relevance of the research was not attempted by two out of the team of seven, while two of them tried only to some extent. The issue of colleague "buy in" is echoed here as seen earlier. For six out of the seven, the research did spark more discussion on staff, while one was not aware of any more staff discussion on the issue. Three of the seven team members reported tension among staff as a result of the research, though it is not clear whether the cause of the tension was the research issue or the actual data gathering process. Six research team members felt that their school should do more research projects. There was no response from the seventh.

The way forward—potential of school administrators to foster data-driven decision-making in their schools

If schools' decision-making is to be driven by evidence, school leaders must have the capacity to facilitate the collection and analysis of data. Eight school administrators (in some schools, both principal and vice-principal) provided responses to a questionnaire which generated the data presented in Table 1.2.

Surprisingly, only three of the eight administrators indicated that they had definitely studied research formally, and four "sort of." One of them said "no." To be appointed as a vice principal or a principal, a teacher must have completed the postgraduate Diploma in Education in which one of the four courses is a research project supported by a research methods module. It seems, then, that some of the graduates of this program do not feel sufficiently equipped to either conduct or to guide research. Four of them felt confident that they understood how to conduct formal research while the other four said they "sort of" understood.

With regard to their administrative skills to implement research in their schools, at least half of them had challenges with support from teachers, and all of them found lack of time to be an obstacle. An apparent contradiction seems to be that whereas all of them indicated that there were reasons which prevented them from conducting or implementing research in their schools, they all reported that they could get teachers to work collaboratively on research in school. Clearly, on the one hand,

TABLE 1.2 *School administrators' potential to foster DDDM in their schools*

	No. of school administrators out of 8		
	Yes	No	Sort of
Academic capability			
I have formally studied research methodology	3	1	4
I understand how to conduct research formally	4		4
Administrative skills			
I know how to factor research into teachers' schedule	6	1	1
Lack of time prevents me from conducting research	1		7
Lack of collegial support prevents me from conducting research		5	3
Lack of support from teachers prevents me from conducting research		4	4
I can get teachers to work collaboratively on research at school	8		
There should be more professional development workshops at school	7		1
Research orientedness			
I conduct my own formal research in school		5	3
I forms teams among staff to conduct research at school	3	1	4
I know there is always existing data that I can use to better understand teaching and learning in my own context	8		
Willingness to learn			
I would like to find out how to conduct research in school in an efficient and practical way	6		2
I think this research would be useful to me in my own leadership position	7		1

DOI: 10.1057/9781137412393.0005

they feel capable of doing this, but on the other, this feeling may not always be translated into action. Similarly, they all felt that there should be more professional development workshops at their school. One would think that as administrators of their schools, they would have some measure of control over this as opposed to merely hoping that it would happen. There seems to be a gap between recognizing a general need for professional development, formalizing the need and filling the need. The gap may be the lack of understanding of the role of the administrator.

Five of the eight administrators do not conduct any formal research in their schools, while three do sometimes. All are aware of existing data that can be used for meaningful research, and seven form staff teams to conduct research. They are all willing to learn how to conduct research in their school in an efficient and practical way, and they all thought that this research project would be useful to them in their own leadership position. When the results of the research were presented to the staff, one vice-principal commented in the feedback: "Thank you for a most informative session—the data presented will be very useful for both administration and staff. Follow-up research is very important." A principal wrote: "The findings of this research have in some instances been an eye-opener. It gives me a better understanding of the behaviour of some of our students."

The feedback from the school administrators leaves one to conclude that due to the diverse levels of administrative and research capability and implementation, there does not exist a school culture that is committed to institutionalized data-driven decision-making. While there is evidence of some occurrence, such as the use of examination results, there is no *common* understanding, approach nor commitment to formally gathering and analyzing data to inform professional practice in any of the schools. No system has emerged from this research project. Perhaps a different research approach would elicit supplemental findings.

Discussion and conclusion

The purpose of this study was to examine the research culture in five secondary schools in a developing country by determining their openness and readiness to use data to make decisions in their school settings. These schools operate in a context where data-driven decision-making is not imposed by any governmental or national body unlike most schools in the First World nations. If schools use data, it is likely for localized reasons and in informal ways. This context is reminiscent of education systems where teachers' perspectives were not present in research efforts which lead to reform (Butt et al., 1992).

In this study, although the research teams and administrators demonstrated some interest in the concept of a research intervention in their school, the challenge of harnessing the teams demonstrated that structures were not in place for this type of activity. Team work and "buy-in" were not always evident since large percentages of teachers were not aware of the project in their schools. Yet many teachers in all schools would have liked to have been on a research team, and most teachers felt that more research projects should be done in their schools. It was also clear that there were definite issues which teachers could identify for investigation. The dilemma of this study was that while the topics chosen for investigation were selected by the school, the initial idea for the research was externally imposed. This in part supports Ohi's (2008) concern that the teacher input may be the missing link in the research–policy–praxis nexus. The research teams' high level of interest in the topics generated by themselves supports Bevan's (2004) view that teachers are motivated by what is useful to them in their daily experience and situation. Even though the teams selected topics which they felt were pertinent to their own schools, none of these topics required data that were already collected by the school. Many teachers reported (67%) that their school research has to do with test/exam results but many more (81%) reported that they used data other than test results. Many more teachers reported conducting informal research as opposed to formal research. So any lack of interest or enthusiasm for this particular research project may have stemmed from the extra effort teachers would have had to make to provide feedback through questionnaires, or to pay attention to what the team was engaged in.

In these five schools, *outcome* data (Marsh et al., 2006) were more the norm than *perception* data (Bernhardt 2003, 2004, 2005), yet when given the opportunity to investigate an issue, all five issues required perception data from both teachers and students. In each case, the team's passion about the research topic pointed to their hope that their findings would influence internal school policy. We recall that most of the teachers in general reported that they use the results of their own research to inform their teaching, with informal research being more predominant than informal. For each school, one challenge of using the findings of this research may be the school's questioning of its validity unless its use involves high stakes (Marsh et al., 2006). It is yet to be seen whether these results would factor into any decision-making in these schools.

Marsh et al. (2006) had cited staff capacity for research as a factor determining research engagement in schools. Do these five schools have the teacher capacity to conduct research effectively? Most of the teachers had studied research formally and claimed to understand how to conduct research including how to analyze data. Most of them also were aware that there is always existing data to use for making decisions. One limitation evident except in the case of one school was ease of collaboration with colleagues. This would be an impediment to the professional learning communities and the culture of collaboration which are germane to data-driven decision-making according to Chen et al. (2005), Holcomb (2001), Love (2004), and Symonds (2003). Nevertheless, there appears to be sufficient capacity to begin the research process.

Such capability to use data to make decisions is matched with a high percentage of teachers who want to find out how to conduct research in an efficient and practical way. Most of them would also like "buy in" from their entire staff and administration where school research is involved. These factors augur well for the schools' potential for data-driven decision-making especially as most found this research project to be useful for whole school development and for their own teaching. With reasonable capability and potential, what is missing in the reality of these schools that would enable research-based decision-making?

Gordon (2004) has concluded that principals as transformational leaders are essential to an effective research-engaged school. What was interesting is that some principals did not feel that they had the requisite research skills and even when they knew how to manage collaboration among staff, they often did not. For both teachers and administrators, time was a factor that impeded them from conducting research in a formal way. This is in keeping with the work of Feldman and Tung (2001) and Ingram et al., (2004), who reported that allocating and providing time for teachers to consistently examine and reflect on data was a challenge for most schools. The "competent system" of Zmuda et al. (2004) may need to be adopted by these schools, and while the principals felt that there should be more professional workshops to develop capacity in their schools, it appears that principals themselves need to seek help to develop those managerial skills needed to take their schools forward out of the syndrome of what could be perceived to be stagnation. Since these five schools are recognized nationally as high-performing schools, it was interesting to note that only one of the five topics had to do with student achievement explicitly. This points to the reality that there are issues in these schools that require further probing and critical inquiry. Perhaps they now need to extend their focus from simply innovating teaching and learning strategies and resources to examining some deeper and perceived "peripheral" issues such as the ones highlighted in this research project: teacher gender, subject selection systems, pressure on students to excel, student motivation, and school culture. The philosophy of openness and collaboration advocated by Detert et al. (2000), Mason (2002), Lachat and Smith (2005), and Mieles and Foley (2005) would ensure that the voices of teachers are heard and that appropriate action is taken for the ultimate fulfillment of their school's vision.

What the research teams had to say about their involvement in the project provides a useful summary that could guide school leaders in their journey to becoming transformational leaders in schools fuelled by data-driven decision-making. There was evidence showing that teachers want to develop their research skills; they want to probe their own school issues; they recognize that any single issue has relevance for students' benefit; they see the need to share their own findings with their counterpart schools at least; they are excited by the prospect of researching their own school issues; they appreciate a spirit of cooperation, openness, and expertise among leaders and members involved in the research effort.

Teachers in this context face a dilemma. Though they are generally aware of the need to use data to make decisions and are interested in conducting research in their own school settings, the infrastructural conditions necessary to enable them to do this, such as time and organized teamwork are lacking. It would be worthwhile to investigate the kinds of informal research that they engage in, and to follow up on the principals' need to know how to conduct research in their schools in an efficient and practical way by providing professional support. Such a combination of interventions may prove to be a useful collaborative effort between school and university.

Note

1 Author's journal.

References

Altrichter, H., Posch, P., & Somekh, B. (1993). *Teachers Investigate Their Work: An Introduction to the Methods of Action Research*. London: Routledge.

Bernhardt, V. (2003). *Using Data to Improve Student Learning in Elementary Schools*. Larchmont, NY: Eye on Education.

Bernhardt, V. (2004). *Using Data to Improve Student Learning in Middle Schools*. Larchmont, NY: Eye on Education.

Bernhardt, V. (2005). *Using Data to Improve Student Learning in High Schools*. Larchmont, NY: Eye on Education.

Bevan, R. M. (2004). Filtering, fragmenting, and fiddling? Teachers' life cycles, and phases in their engagement with research. *Teacher Development, 8*, 2 & 3.

Butt, R., Raymond, D., McCue, G., & Yamagishi, L. (1992). Collaborative autobiography and the teacher's voice. In Goodson, I. (Ed.) *Studying Teachers' Lives*. London: Routledge.

Chen, E., Heritage, M., & Lee, J. (2005). Identifying and monitoring students' learning needs with technology. *Journal of Education for Students Placed at Risk, 10*, 3, 309–332.

Choppin, J. (2002). "Data Use in Practice: Examples from the School Level," paper presented at the Annual Conference of the American Educational Research Association, New Orleans, La.

Clandinin, D., & Connelly, M. (1995). *Teachers' Professional Knowledge Landscapes*. New York: Teachers College Press.

Coburn, C., Honig, M. I., & Stein, M. K. (2005). *What's the Evidence on Districts' Use of Evidence?* Chapter prepared for conference volume, sponsored by the MacArthur Network on Teaching and Learning.

Darling-Hammond, L., & Ascher, C. (1991). *Creating Accountability in Big City School Systems. Urban Diversity Series # 102*. New York: ERIC Clearinghouse on Urban Education.

De Lisle, J., Seecharan, H., & Ayodike, A. T. (2010). Is Trinidad and Tobago education system structured to facilitate optimum human capital development? New findings on the relationship between education structures and outcomes from national and international assessments. In *10th SALISES Annual Conference*, Cave Hill, Barbados. Retrieved from: http://sta.uwi.edu/conferences/09/salises/documents/J%20De%20Lisle.pdf.

Detert, J. R., Kopel, M. E. B., Mauriel, J.J. & Jenni, . W. (2000). "Quality Management in U.S. High Schools: Evidence from the Field," *Journal of School Leadership, 10,* 158–187.

Feldman, J., & Tung, R. (2001). "Whole School Reform: How Schools Use the Data-Based Inquiry and Decision Making Process," paper presented at the 82nd Annual Meeting of the American Educational Research Association, Seattle, Washington.

Goodson, I. F., & Hargreaves, A. (Eds.) (1996). *Teachers' Professional Lives.* London: Falmer Press.

Gordon, S. P. (2004). *Professional Development for School Improvement: Empowering Learning Communities.* Boston: Allyn & Bacon.

Government of Trinidad and Tobago (GORTT) (2009). Vision 2020 Operational Plan 2007–2010, 2008–2009 Progress Report. Ministry of Planning, Housing and the Environment. Government of the Republic of Trinidad and Tobago. Port-of-Spain, Trinidad.

Handscomb, G., & MacBeath, J. (2003). *The Research Engaged School,* Chelmsford, Forum for Learning and Research Enquiry (FLARE), Essex County Council.

Hargreaves, D. (1998). "The Knowledge-creating School", paper presented at British Educational Research Association Conference, Belfast.

Holcomb, E.L. (2001). *Asking the Right Questions: Techniques for Collaboration and School Change* (2nd edn). Thousand Oaks, CA: Corwin.

Ingram, D., Seashore Louis, K., & Schroeder, R. D. (2004). Accountability policies and teacher decision making: barriers to the use of data to improve practice. *Teachers College Record, 106,* 6, 2004, pp. 1258–1287.

Lachat, M.A., & Smith, S. (2005). Practices that support data use in urban high schools. *Journal of Education for Students Placed at Risk, 10,* 3, 333–349.

Lashway, L. (2001). Educational Indicators. Eugene, Oregon: *ERIC Clearinghouse on Educational Management,* University of Oregon.

Love, N. (2004). Taking data to new depths. *JSD, 25,* 4, Fall. http://www.nsdc.org/library/publications/jsd/love254.cfm

Mandinach, E., Honey, M., Light, D., & Brunner, C. (January 2008). a conceptual framework for data-driven decision-making. In E. Mandinach & M. Honey (Eds), *Data-Driven School Improvement:*

Linking Data and Learning (pp. 13–31). New York: Teachers College Press.

Marsh, J. A., Pane, J. F., & Hamilton. L. S. (2006). *Making Sense of Data-Driven Decision Making in Education: Evidence from Recent RAND Research.* Santa Monica, CA: RAND Corporation, 2006. http://www.rand.org/pubs/occasional_papers/OP170.

Mason, S. (2002). *Turning Data into Knowledge: Lessons from Six Milwaukee Public Schools.* Madison, WI: Wisconsin Center for Education Research.

Mieles, T. & Foley, E. (2005). *From Data to Decisions: Lessons from School Districts Using Data Warehousing.* Providence, RI: Annenberg Institute for School Reform at Brown University.

National College for School Leadership (NCSL) (2006). Leading a Research-engaged School. www.nfer.ac.uk/research-areas/research-engaged-schools/becoming-a-researchengaged- school.cfm.

Ohi, S. (2008). The teacher's role in the research-policy-praxis nexus. *Australian Journal of Education*, 52, 1, 95–109, Australian Council for Educational Research, Sydney, N.S.W.

Roberts, B. (2002). *Biographical Research.* Buckingham, UK: Open University Press.

Sharp, C., Eames, A., Sanders, D., & Tomlinson, K. (2005). *Postcards from Research engaged Schools*, Slough, NFER.

Shen, J., Cooley, V., Reeves, P., Burt, W., Ryan, L., Rainey, J. M., & Yuan, W. (2010). Using data for decision-making: perspectives from 16 principals in Michigan, USA. *International Review of Education*, 56, 435–456.

Supovitz, J. A., & Klein, V. (2003). *Mapping Course for Improved Student Learning: How Innovative Schools Systematically Use Student Performance Data to Guide Improvement*, Philadelphia, PA: Consortium for Policy Research in Education, University of Pennsylvania Graduate School of Education.

Wilson, E. (1972). Can the school become a center of inquiry? In *Perspectives for Reform in Education*, Bruce Joyce and Marsha Weil (Eds), Columbia University Teachers' College. Englewood Cliffs, NJ. Prentice-Hall Inc.

Zmuda, A., Kuklis, R., & Kline, E. (2004). *Transforming Schools: Creating a Culture of Continuous Improvement.* Alexandria, VA: Association for Supervision and Curriculum Development.

2
The Challenge of Maintaining School Culture in a Traditional School Setting—A Case Study

Abstract: *This report presents the findings of research conducted in an all girls traditional secondary school (School R) in Trinidad. It sought to ascertain the views of teachers, students, and parents on school culture including traditionally held beliefs, values, and practices. Interviews with teachers, deans, a past administrator, and questionnaire responses from 116 parents and 73 students of varying levels of the school indicated that certain values and cherished traditions are still valued by the majority of stakeholders. Parents' views indicate the need for more communication and collaboration among the school's major stakeholders. Parents and students suggested enabling students to cope at school, teacher attitudes and strategies, maintaining standards of discipline, what students should learn, and enabling a sense of belonging as ways of maintaining student excellence.*

Yamin-Ali, Jennifer. *Data-Driven Decision-Making in Schools: Lessons from Trinidad.* New York: Palgrave Macmillan, 2014. DOI: 10.1057/9781137412393.0006.

Introduction and background

No matter what the geographical, political, or socio-cultural context, the notion of school culture has been the focus of discussion and enquiry by scholars and practitioners worldwide.

It is often said that the school is a microcosm of the wider society. A consequence of this phenomenon would be that as society changes so would behaviors and attitudes among the school population. Those residing within a school over time would no doubt have been sufficiently convinced that their beliefs and practices are worthy of maintaining, whereas newcomers to the system (either new teachers or new students and their parents) may perhaps not "fit in" with the culture of the school at some or all levels. Such disharmony among stakeholders' fundamental beliefs could provide a threat to an institution anchored in tradition and convinced in its established culture.

School culture is an issue for school leaders at each level. Lumby and Foskett (2011) maintain that current interest in culture remains strong, to some extent because of the increasing awareness that education faces the challenges of technological, economic, and social change. They suggest that a revisiting of cultural values is essential when one considers the implications of practice and power relations brought about by change itself and an inability to deal with it.

School culture, put in simple terms, may be defined as *"the way we do things around here"* according to Deal (1993). Moving beyond this simple definition, school culture encompasses the basic assumptions and beliefs shared by the members of a school regarding things such as human nature, human activity, and human relationships. Conor and Lake (1988) explain that at the surface layer, culture relates to things such as physical settings, language, and stories, while at a deeper layer, it refers to the ceremonies/customs and symbols (such as uniforms and logos) as well as the accepted standards of behavior (rules and procedures). At the deepest layer, culture refers to such things as the fundamental assumptions and core values of both individuals and the organization.

The context of the school in this case study is one where historically, education has been a key contributory factor in social mobility. It is a post-colonial developing nation where currently, students access secondary schools based on their performance in a qualifying examination. Thus, there is much competition based on academic performance. It is perceived that the quality of education varies from school to school. For most of the population, educational achievement is the key to their "success". There is consequently a great deal of competition to attend what they perceive to be the best schools.

The school under study is considered a "first choice school" in Trinidad due to its track record of high academic achievement and students' involvement in extra- and co-curricular activities. "First choice" is determined by the number of students selecting it as their first choice of placement in the Secondary Entrance Assessment (SEA). The school was established in 1950 by Canadian missionaries. Christian standards and values still undergird the school's mission.

The school offers a seven year program of study to girls aged eleven to nineteen, and the students come from diverse social, cultural and religious backgrounds. Its mission describes the school as a "family with its rich history of tradition" which "teaches concern and respect for all and the acceptance of responsibility for our actions." The school also seeks to nurture "articulate, confident, empowered individuals who as critical thinkers and life-long learners will make a positive impact on society" (School's website). Many school traditions have been maintained over the years, including the support of loyal alumnae. Its symbols, such as its uniform, are a major part of its culture.

The school competes with others for national scholarships and parents and students expect high standards of the school, while teachers have high of expectations of students' attitudes, behavior, and performance. They also expect high levels of cooperation from parents.

Changes in social norms, however, are sometimes a challenge to the expectations of guardians of the traditional norms. School administrators and teachers globally have therefore been encountering disillusion and dismay as standards of behavior which were previously commonly valued, are now viewed as old-fashioned or meaningless. It is in the context of changes in school culture that some teachers of this school felt a strong concern that the culture of the school was being eroded by new patterns of behavior and attitudes observed in some students at the school.

New patterns of behavior and attitudes are to be expected in dynamic organizations and "living spaces" such as schools. According to Silins et al. (2002, p. 24), "schools are feeling this tidal wave of change in ways that 'have left many educators – consciously or otherwise – confused, exhausted and disillusioned'" (citing Deal, 1990, p. 31). Schools which function in a mechanistic mode will find great difficulty in dealing with the challenge of emergent cultures within what has come to be known as the "normal" culture within a school.

The culture of a school, according to Peterson in Apple Learning Exchange (2008, p. 107), "has a personality of its very own...some cherished traditions, unwritten rules, unspoken expectations, a proud heritage or past, and a sense of spirit". Further comments on school culture include Bush's (1995, p. 29) comment that culture refers to the "values, beliefs and norms of individuals in the organisation" and is "manifested by symbols and rituals rather than through the formal structure of an organisation." In addition to these views, Hoyle (1986, p. 150) sees ritual at the centre of school culture, claiming that "symbols are the key components of all schools" and they have "expressive tasks and symbols which are the only means whereby abstract values can be conveyed...Symbols are central to the process of conveying meaning." In fact, culture is seen to be integral to the curriculum offered by a school, but it is a "hidden curriculum" according to Owens (1987, p. 168), who sees such a curriculum as "the values that are transmitted literally from one generation to another."

If schools are concerned with values transmission, alongside academic preparation, we need to consider to what extent this thinking is reflected in the literature on school quality. Regarding the school as a learning organization, school culture is normally included as one of the factors contributing to organizational learning. Leithwood, Leonard, and Sharratt (1998) identified collaborative and collegial school cultures as a necessary condition for fostering organizational learning. But more often than not, such collaboration is usually viewed from a staff perspective. In as much as parents and students are major stakeholders in the education process, we must recognize that they have a role to play in successful schooling. The Character Education Partnership (CEP) (2010) defines a positive school culture as one that includes "the schoolwide ethos and the culture of individual classrooms, high expectations for learning and achievement, a safe and caring environment, shared values and relational trust, a powerful pedagogy and curriculum, high student motivation and engagement, a professional faculty culture, and partnerships with families and the community" (p. 1). This CEP position paper claims that the best schools in America, apart from having very dedicated educators, have school cultures that "foster excellence and moral character" (p. 2). The paper goes on to define "character" as including "both 'moral character'—treating others well (through kindness, honesty and respect)—and 'performance character', doing things well." CEP has used research based data to derive Eleven Principles of Effective Character Education. These principles assume

> a school culture that demands and supports ethical virtue and citizenship while providing an instructional environment that demands and supports best academic effort through challenging work and high expectations.
>
> These Eleven Principles include intentionally fostering moral and performance character through every phase of school life, developing a caring school community, creating an engaging academic curriculum, promoting shared school leadership, and involving families and the community as partners. (p. 3)

Peterson in Apple Learning Exhange (2008) delineates some major features of positive school culture as being a shared sense of purpose which is widely shared by staff members, an emphasis on continuous learning and improvement in the school, a sense of responsibility for students' learning, collaborative and collegial relationships, as also espoused by Leithwood et al. (1998), and attention to professional development, staff reflection, and sharing of professional practice. What is also interesting about Peterson's comments on positive school culture is that he mentions details such as "grass and flowers," "clean and neat," visible "school mission," "live plants," "mottos," "messages...on the walls, in the classrooms, in the main office." In other words, school climate is inextricably linked to school culture. The CEP (2010), in their discussion of school culture, points out that the National School Climate Council (NSCC) of the U.S. uses "school climate" in a similar way to how CEP uses the term "school culture" to cover a broad range of factors within the school environment that have to do with the physical, emotional, social, ethical, civic, and intellectual domains of schooling. According to CEP, a broadly conceived positive school culture includes:

- social climate;
- intellectual climate;
- rules and policies that hold all school members accountable to high standards of learning and behavior;
- traditions and routines;
- structures that facilitate staff and student voice and shared responsibility;
- effective partnering with parents;

▸ norms for relationships and behaviour. ("Developing and Assessing School Culture—A New Level of Accountability for Schools", p. 6, CEP)

They also report that in new urban schools, social courtesy is included in their treatment of school culture.

Proponents of character education are convinced that it has the power to change lives (Elbot & Fulton, 2008; Lickona, Shaps & Lewis, 1995; Kilpatrick, 1992), and according to CEP "when students enter a culture that demands and supports quality work and moral character, they tend to fit into that culture" (2010, p. 4).

There is some concern, however, about the conceptualization of "character education" as it fits into the paradigm of school culture. The concern, in summary, surrounds the style of moral training that programs may employ, as well as the values they may promote which will be based on assumptions about students' nature and how they learn. Fundamentally, if schools promote values which are not in the best interest of all, then the effort is flawed. Kohn (1997) critiques approaches to character education which do not enable a lasting commitment to wholesome values. He cautions against the potential of extrinsic motivation to erode intrinsic motivation to "be good", basically. He is also critical of the goals or agendas of some proponents of character education. He questions conventional norms of "good" behavior as does Purpel (1991). He also quotes another skeptic who describes the character education movement as "a yearning for some halcyon days of moral niceties and social tranquility" (Lockwood, 1991, p. 246 as cited in Kohn, 1997).

Shaping one's character and having that character "fit into" the culture of a school has so much to do with one's own "baggage"—one's own personal experiences. According to Hinde (2004) teachers' "personal experiences, values, norms, and prior education all influence their views of curriculum, pedagogy and change even before they set foot into a classroom. Any change that is proposed that runs counter to the teachers' already-developed culture and philosophy will be resisted" (p. 4). Hinde's view is consistent with those of Sarason who says that "because our values and assumptions are usually implicit and 'second nature', we proceed as if the way things are is the way things should or could be" (pp. 136–137). For example, Finnan (2000) identified five underlying assumptions that influence the success or failure of school reform. Such assumptions include our views on respect for students, on the meaning of "democratic education", on adults in schools and parents, on rituals and procedures and whether they suit the educational needs of students, and on reasons for the choice of "best practices". A final assumption involves how change is viewed by the school community.

The examining of the notion of "school culture" involves the consideration of "perpetuation" versus "development". In this chapter, it is an issue that emerges especially as Sarason (1996) reminds us that teachers tend to teach the way they have been taught. If their exposure has been characterized by power relationships that are hierarchical and dictatorial, then students and parents would be denied the opportunity to ask many questions, to present opposing views, or to feel a sense of ownership of direction and decisions.

"Perpetuation" may make it an overwhelming challenge to face Kohn's daring critique (1997) of how traditional schools view the ideal student. He questions the notion of the "loyal, patriotic, obedient" student as opposed to the "empathic and sceptical" one. He cites de Charms (1983) as he endorses the value of true student autonomy where students come to see themselves as "origins" rather than "pawns." Kohn's questioning of the status quo regarding values and philosophies challenges school communities to reflect with a view to transformation. He calls for dissection of problems in order that they be solved from the inside out.

Such dissection of problems calls our attention back to the complexity theory mentioned earlier. Fong (2006) suggests that factors such as communication, feedback, human relations, collaboration, mutual respect and support, lifelong learning, teamwork and interaction are important for complexity-driven changes. Complexity theory suggests that it is necessary to consciously prepare staff for changes, enabling them to cope with the dynamism of problems and issues by adapting in an interactive way. Their individual new capabilities can create a ripple effect for dealing with challenges internal and external to the school as an organization.

In a sense, this research has provided the opportunity for such dissection to take place, but it is only the beginning. The initial concern that drove this research initiative is itself a major factor in the evaluation and discussion of school culture in the given context.

Methodology

A descriptive case study approach was employed in this research which is a single case featuring both qualitative and quantitative methodologies.

The focus of this case study is on the contemporary phenomenon of school culture within its real-life context. Boundaries between the phenomenon and its context are hazy due to the nature of school culture and the many psycho-social factors that impact it. This study follows the description of case study research by Yin (1994), who points out that this approach is suitable for studying complex social phenomena as is the case of this study.

Within the case study paradigm, this study uses an embedded design thereby including multiple units of analysis. Within the same case the intention was to look for consistent patterns of evidence across units.

The questions guiding the study were:

1. How is the school's culture defined and described within the school community?
2. Why do parents and students view the school as a 1st choice school?
3. What are the systems in place to maintain school culture?
4. What are students' views on the details of the school's current culture?
5. What are parents' views on the details of the school's current culture?
6. What are parents' and students' views on creating and maintaining "excellence" in students at the school?

The context of the study is an all girls secondary school affiliated to the Presbyterian Church. It is largely government financed. It has over 60 years of a tradition that embraces conservative values and practices. It has maintained high achievement over the decades, and has consistently promoted and facilitated holistic development through a wide variety of extra and co-curricular activities.

Data collection was initiated when the researcher was seeking to initiate a culture of data-driven decision-making at the school. She initially interviewed a combination of five teachers from the school to ascertain any major area of concern they had with regard to any aspect of school life in their context. The teachers agreed that a major concern for them was the subtle and gradual erosion of what they conceived to be elements of the school culture. This concern translated into the need to find out the views of students and parents about elements that evidently composed the school's culture.

The researcher then created a research plan with the team, designed all the data collection instruments, and shared it with the team for their input. The researcher also studied the school's student handbook which delineates the school's motto, expectations from students, and rules and regulations. This document, along with the two focus group interviews with the research team, an interview with two deans of the school, and an interview with a past long-standing principal of the school informed the design of two separate questionnaires for random parents and students throughout the school. The researcher's understanding of the context also contributed to the content of the questionnaire.

Teachers administered the student questionnaire, which was filled out at school (N73) and the parent questionnaire was sent out to approximately 120 parents with 116 being completed. Both questionnaires were completed anonymously to ensure that parties felt comfortable to be open with their opinions and views.

Both questionnaires were almost identical except for changes in wording to suit the respondent (either parent or student). For the question concerning school rules, only controversial ones were included in the parents' questionnaire so as not to overburden the instrument with items.

The use of teacher, dean, and past principal interviews, student and parent questionnaires, and examination of the school handbook allowed for triangulation which enhanced the construct validity of the research.

Quantitative analysis was applied for the closed-ended questions. Patterns and trends were sought through that analysis as well. Some comparison and deeper insights into phenomena were achieved through cross-analysis. For the open-ended questions recurring themes were recognized and categorized repeatedly until comprehensive but clear categories were established without losing the voices of the respondents. Comparison of responses within groups and across groups allowed for deeper analysis.

Findings are presented below according to the research questions.

Findings

Teachers' understanding of the concept of "school culture"

Interviews with two deans of the school revealed that for them school culture had to do with "traditions, the whole atmosphere pervading throughout... teachers, students, so that when students come here you want them to recognize what values we have, what is important to the school as a whole."

They also felt that the school's culture and how the school was perceived had a lot to do with the reality that generations within the same family attended the school in large enough numbers to perpetuate the spirit and the customs of the school.

In a discussion with five young teachers, four of whom were past students of the school, one expressed the view that "culture was more than just rules and a handbook. From 8.15 to 2.15, it's about how to behave in an appropriate manner. In our time we never had a handbook...we fell into a behaviour...I don't remember anyone telling us about these things...we knew...we saw other students doing it...that's the way and we knew it."

A long-standing retired principal who contributed significantly to the growth of the school from the early years said that if the concept of "culture" is seen as "a veneer...a polish," then practices can't last "over a period of time." Believing that "worship is the basis of all spirituality and discipline" and that "we have to build on spirituality," she saw the school in her tenure as "a family school." She also managed the teaching staff through her conviction that "people have to lead by example."

Why parents and students view the school as a 1st choice school

The four most common reasons parents and students expressed when asked why they thought the school was a first choice school were "discipline," "all-rounded education," "academic results and quality of teaching" and "environment." Some respondents offered multiple reasons. "All-rounded education" included comments about the school's inclusion of extra-curricular activities in its offerings. Extended comments on the school environment included words such as "caring", "tolerant", "respect", "safety", "family-like", and "bond among girls". What is interesting is that significantly higher percentages of students than parents cited "all-rounded education" (or extra-curricular activities) and "environment" as a reason for the school being a first choice school. It may well be that it is because these features of the students' firsthand experience of school life impact their impression of the school. Parents' impressions are as observers or they rely on second hand information, whereas the lived experiences of the students would account for more than the parent is aware of.

Small numbers of parents and students mentioned reasons including values, spirituality, school history/reputation, physical amenities, uniform, and traditions.

Systems to maintain school culture

Discussions with teachers, including deans, indicated that the students' handbook was an integral document used within the school system to regulate students' behavior which they feel should be undergirded by certain treasured values. In their initial discussion of the issue of school culture, the team of five young teachers had raised the issue of "lack of respect and discipline" among students as a cause for concern, especially when they compared their own experience as students at the school with the current students. Although they acknowledge that "the school culture is deeper than the handbook," this research sought to find out to what extent the students and parents agreed with the school rules as stated in the school's handbook.

Although generally most parents and students agreed with all the school rules, the rule which the largest number of students and parents disagreed with had to do with school uniform. With regard to how socks are worn, 10 parents and 17 students opposed this rule citing a variety of reasons. Eight parents and six students did not agree that high top sneakers should not be worn. Their reasons were also varied, mainly practical, pointing out that it's just a shoe, and correct color and cleanliness were the important factors.

Ten parents also did not agree with the rule that no electronic devices should be allowed in the classroom other than laptops. The reasons given included usefulness as a teaching/learning tool and for relaxation.

Nine parents and six students did not agree that students must stand to speak in class. Those parents responded in these ways: "You don't need to stand to show someone you respect them," "It depends on the exercise in progress. If it's team work then you need to be seated," "What's the point? It makes more sense to raise your hand and wait for the teacher to call you to answer while seated," "Not necessarily all the time," "It depends on the teacher or the student may feel intimidated when standing," "May cause embarrassment. It's better for them to sit and answer," "This does not show respect." Some of these responses were echoed in the responses of students, six of whom disagreed with the rule: "Standing would make children feel uncomfortable and shy," "Students may get embarrassed," "It makes shy persons very uncomfortable." Seven parents did not think it was necessary for students to stand when a teacher enters the classroom. Some reasons offered were: "It should all be great if students simply greet their teachers," "If teacher leaves and returns 5 times, what then," "Teachers are not royalty," "Chairs scraping the ground is not nice." Only three students indicated that standing when a teacher enters the classroom was not important.

More parents than students agreed that nails should be short without nail polish and that no accessories are allowed apart from those stipulated. Three parents and seven students disagreed.

Since it seemed that some school rules would obviously be supported by parents (due to bias on researcher's part), opinion was sought from students only. One of these rules was that there should be no eating in class. Sixteen students did not agree with this rule citing several practical reasons including "Some kids don't get time to eat," "Students have eating problems at specific times," "If someone is hungry they should be allowed to eat," "On mornings it should be allowed for those who have missed breakfast."

What parents value regarding daughters' behavior in the school context

Courtesy and politeness

Parents generally indicated that they valued to a great extent or to some extent courtesy and respect as outlined in the school rules. One parent hardly valued being polite to other students, expressing the view that some children can be very disrespectful and rude while another said that some teachers are rude, justifying why students should not be polite to teachers.

Nineteen parents felt that they valued "to some extent" showing consideration for others on the stairs and corridors. No explanations were given. Twenty-eight valued "to some extent", and four "hardly", lining up in two lines and quietly going to assembly. Explanations given by three persons had to do with where the student's classroom is located so "she does not always hear the bell and has to rush to assembly," and another three justified lack of order and silence by the students' need to be close to their friends.

Diligence

While overall, parents valued diligent practices in their daughters, not all valued some of the behaviors "to a great extent". No reasons were given for selecting "to some extent" as opposed to "to a great extent" for "making a careful note of all homework". However, one reason given for hardly valuing doing all homework before it is due is that "there is always a test or a project," signifying that sometimes students do not have time to do all homework. In addition, although most parents felt that their daughters should find out about homework given when they were absent, one parent who did not value this indicated that it was the teachers' job to assist students with the information.

Being a positive role model for other students

Only four parents hardly valued or did not value at all their daughters being a positive role model for other students but did not offer any explanation. Twenty-three valued it to some extent. It cannot be conclusive that being a role model means following the school rules since in some cases, logical reasons were provided for not agreeing with some of them. Emerging from the data, therefore, is the issue of a role model having varying meanings for different people.

Involvement of parents/guardians in school life

Most parents or guardians valued their involvement in their daughters' school life to varying extents. No explanation was given for their choices.

Singing the school hymn with pride

Most parents valued singing the school hymn with pride. The main reason given by the four parents for not valuing it much was religious. This shows that those parents are not aware that the school hymn is not a religious hymn but a hymn of loyalty to the philosophy and values of the school. Perhaps the term "school song" should have been used in the questionnaire.

Students' behavior in terms of school rules

Students were asked to indicate to what extent they practiced certain types of behavior which were listed on the questionnaire.

Courtesy and politeness

With the exception of one student who reported that she was hardly ever polite to other students, all students indicated that they were polite to other students with more than half of the respondents doing so all of the time. Four of the students who were not always polite expressed a view similar to the one who said that "this is because some students do not have respect for you no matter how polite you try to be."

All the students were polite to teachers all of the time, except for three who were polite most of the time and one who was polite some of the time. The explanation given by two students for not being polite all of the time is captured in the comment that "some teachers' attitude affects how I speak to them" and "the same respect I get they receive." There was no apparent difficulty with being polite to the rest of the school community although 14 students said they were "most of the time" as opposed to "all of the time". No comment was made regarding this behavior.

Six students were quiet and attentive at assembly only some of the time and the following explanations were given: "short attention span," "my attention would be at 100% if worship was interesting," "because you would like to ask your friends little questions or discuss what the person is talking about," "assembly is sometimes boring and sometimes I may have better things to talk about."

Seven students raised a hand to ask or answer a question in class only some of the time. Reasons given for this infrequency were: "Mainly because I am quiet, so I just listen to what others say," "there are many students, everyone has a turn," "most questions are asked during an informal discussion," "most of the time I understand the topic being taught and I may not have the answers sometimes," "do not feel to," "It is unnecessary in some classes where interaction is high and common."

All students said that they showed consideration for others on the stairs and corridors and knocked and waited at the office door before entering more often than some of the time.

A relatively large number of students (12/73) line up in two lines and go to assembly quietly less frequently than most of the time. The explanations offered for this infrequency were: "because half of the class comes late/talking," "because some of our class is lazy," "it is hard to line up and be quiet because people are restless on mornings," "hardly anyone does this," "upper six students hardly attend school or usually are late hence too little persons to line up," "old enough to go quietly without lining up."

Students' diligent practice

From their own account, most students engaged in diligent behavior at least most of the time. Those who did so some of the time or hardly offered the following reasons:

For not doing all homework before it is due: "I don't have enough time and I live far away," "difficult at times to finish by due date because of large amount of work," "workload is cumbersome at times to allow completion of assignments."

For not always making a note of all homework, two students indicated that they "have a good memory."

When they do not find out about homework given when they were absent, one student said it is because she "may not always have money on [her] mobile phone."

Being a positive role model for other students

A little more than half of the students said that they were positive role models for other students all of the time. The rest said they were "some of the time". This raises the issue once more of what one perceives to be a role model since the desired behavior by the school administration and teachers in terms of behavior on the way to and at assembly was not practiced by more than 50% of the students. It seems evident that behavior related to assembly needs to be discussed at the school level to clarify its significance to students or to re-orient the administration and students as to its practicality, feasibility, and implementation.

Involvement of parents/guardians in school life

Most students involve their parents or guardians in their school life, but a few gave the following reasons for doing so only some of the time or hardly: "my parents had their time when they were in school," "my parents are very busy," "in order to build independence, children should resolve problems on their own in a responsible way," "we have a mutual understanding that they only need to know about academics due to their busy work schedule." The extent of the involvement is generally in keeping with what parents reported.

Singing the school hymn with pride

Although more than 50% of the students said that they sing the school hymn with pride all the time, 19 do so most of the time, four some of the time and three never do so. Some explained their not singing in the following ways: "music is sometimes hard to follow," "Have no control over sore throat," "pitch is too high at times to sing to," "religious reasons," "I don't sing." "Muslims are not supposed to sing hymns." Two of these reasons indicate that the students misunderstood the question and interpreted "school hymn" as "hymn" rather than "school song".

What parents value re their daughters' attitude in the school context

Relating to others

In terms of relating to others, most parents valued to a great extent positive attitudes in their daughters toward others. The numbers of parents who valued these attitudes to some extent were significantly high, though. In the absence of explanations, it is not possible to understand why they did not select "to a great extent".

Students' selves

Most parents placed a high value on their daughters having a strong sense of self as determined by being willing to accept responsibility for one's action, having high expectations of oneself, and by being interested in one's overall development and not just academic achievement.

Appreciation of school

All parents placed at least a relatively high value on their daughters' appreciation of their school by showing appreciation for the school environment, being proud of their daughter's school, and by being aware that one represents the school as long as one wears the school uniform.

There were some instances of dissonance between what the school would expect and parents' attitudes, evident in the responses that indicate that seven parents appreciate the school environment "to some extent" only, and seven are aware only "to some extent" that one represents the school as long as one wears the uniform.

Students' attitude in terms of school's expectations

Relating to others

While there was a general trend toward relating well to others, there were two areas that stood out as significant. Fourteen students said that it was "most of the time" rather than "all the time" that they were tolerant of the differences between self and others, but no explanation was offered. Eight students reported that they were willing to help others including teachers without rewards while six said they were *never* willing to do so. The latter feedback as well as the moderate lack of tolerance of difference speaks to a need that can perhaps be addressed both in the home and at school since some reservation was also expressed by parents in regard to these attitudes. Nevertheless, one is mindful that respondents were trying to be honest in their responses and that perhaps an interview situation would have elicited clearer feedback on the issues.

Students' selves

Only 74–79% of the student respondents expressed a healthy attitude to "self" in terms of:

- willing to accept responsibility for one's actions;
- having high expectations of oneself;
- being interested in one's overall development and not just academic achievement;
- being proud of one's school;
- being aware that one represents the school as long as one wears the uniform.

What is satisfying though is that no student selected "hardly" or "never" for these attitudes in themselves. In light of the humanness of these attitudes, even "most of the time" could be considered reasonable. One student added the comment "it depends" to the item "willing to accept responsibility for one's actions". Again, this may point to the subjectivity that must be applied to these human responses to situations.

Appreciation of school

There were a significant number of students who show appreciation of school all the time. A relatively large proportion of students (33%) show appreciation of the school environment "most of the time" and not "all the time". One student "hardly" does so. Some students, as many as ten, have lapses in their understanding that the school uniform represents the school. With the exception of seven students, all were proud of their school all of the time. Six were proud of the school "some of the time" and the one who was "never" proud of the school said "because I don't feel special in this school."

Developing and maintaining overall excellence at the school

Parents were asked to indicate whether they agreed that certain factors were important in the developing and maintaining of a highly positive school culture and climate, and students were asked whether they agreed that the statements were important in developing and maintaining overall excellence at the school. The phrase *highly positive school culture and climate* was changed to *overall excellence* since the meaning of the latter may have been easier for students to grasp. The findings are presented according to views on the principal, teachers, and parents, and views on rapport and family spirit at the school.

Principal's behavior and attitude regarding what makes an excellent principal

Parents were asked to respond to the following leadership qualities and behaviors:

- serious about setting high standards of behavior;
- passionate about developing the school in many ways;
- visible in corridors and around the school;
- leads by example in the way she dresses;
- leads by example in her overall behavior and speech;
- leads by example in her overall attitude.

There was almost overall consensus among parents and students that all the statements signify important qualities and behaviors in a principal. However, three parents did not think it was important for the principal to be visible in the corridors and around the school. One of the three felt "it will take away her other duties and many other leadership qualities" and another asked "if she's in the corridor all the time, why would she have an office?"

Two parents did not agree that the principal should lead by example in the way she dresses. Though these did not comment on their opinion, another thought that the principal should "be able to teach students how to dress different without being vulgar." In terms of behavior, one parent recalled an incident in the school when the "behavior was unbecoming of a principal when she found out about a thief in the class."

While all students agreed that it was important for the principal to be visible in the corridors and around the school, one did comment that "the principal has several duties so it is understandable if she cannot do this at all times." Four students did not agree that the way the principal dresses was important. The single comment made was that "clothing has nothing to do with attitude."

In terms of a principal's contribution to a school's overall excellence students commented that "a principal who works hard to get answers to a problem that may exist would gain the respect of all students," and that by walking the corridors "the principal is able to see results, in terms of students obeying rules," that "children hold leaders in high respect thus, a visibly active principal inspires a good student," that a "Principal [should] examine techniques of getting through to children," and that a "Principal—should command respect, not demand respect." One student commented that "passion is the driving force to success, we need passion in this school" and another advised that administration should "stop caring about petty image and nonsense and focus on the holistic development."

Teachers' behaviors and attitudes

Parents and students provided their responses to these teacher behaviors and attitudes:

- teachers who are serious about setting high standards of behavior;
- teachers who lead by example in the way that they dress;
- teachers who lead by example in their overall behavior and speech;
- teachers who lead by example in their overall attitude;
- teachers who devote time to non-academic areas of the school.

With regard to teachers' behavior, attitude, and dress, there was mostly consensus on all the statements except for one parent who did not feel that a highly positive school culture and climate depended on teachers who are serious about setting high standards of behavior. This parent felt that teachers "should be strict but friendly with students." Two parents and two students were of the view that teachers who lead by example in the way they dress was not an important criterion in developing this type of school culture and climate. The single comment made by a student was that, as in the case of the principal, "clothing has nothing to do with attitude." This criterion may have been confusing for one parent who responded that teachers should "be able to teach students how to dress different without being vulgar" and commented on the inappropriate way that some teachers dressed. Perhaps this parent felt that in those cases that example was not a good one to follow.

In their attempt to explain why they agreed with some of the statements above, some students commented that "teachers need to be aware of how they dress as students take notes," that in terms of teachers' involvement in non-academic areas "holistic development encourages kids to dream and persevere," that "attitudes of teachers should always be inspiring and motivating," that "when they (teachers) are friendly, students can speak to them if they have problems."

Parental support and involvement

Only one parent and one student did not agree that parent involvement in the life of the school contributed to either a highly positive school climate and culture or overall excellence at school. No comment was given by the student but the parent qualified his/her answer by saying "to some extent." Two parents and two students did not see that parents who support the school's effort at student discipline and attitude was an important contributor to school culture, but no explanation was given.

Rapport and appreciation

All parents agreed that good rapport between principal and students and between teachers and students is important in this context. One parent justified her support for good rapport between teachers and students by commenting that "challenges can be foreseen and dealt with proactively rather than reactively," and another felt that by ensuring a good rapport between the principal and students, "the student feels a sense of safety around the school."

One parent did not agree that school administration should show appreciation of teachers in an effort toward building school culture and climate, and one student did not agree that this was an important factor in developing overall excellence in a school because "it must be remembered that the ambition and success is the effort of the kids."

Family spirit

Four parents were of the opinion that family spirit at the school was not important in developing school culture and climate, whereas all students agreed that this was an important factor in developing overall excellence in the school.

Students advocated a family spirit at school by saying that with it "there will be a sense of togetherness, students can support each other," "a child feels secure, something they may not have at home," and "at [school] we are always told of the fact that we are sisters."

Other comments

Two additional suggestions from parents for building school climate and culture at the school were that "teachers/principals should acknowledge parents to feel welcome, a raised hand or smile," and a "good PTA (Parent/Teacher Association)."

Student behaviors valued by parents and students

In this category, the question posed to parents varied slightly in its wording from the one posed to students in order to ensure that they were able to relate to the question. The feedback sought was the same. Both questions required the respondents to indicate what student behaviors they valued. The question posed to parents was: "*What are some student behaviors that you think would make your daughter an exemplary [name of school] girl?*" The question to students was: "*What are some of the student behaviors at school that you think are important to making and keeping [name of school] an excellent school?*"

In all, parents mentioned 111 types of behaviors and students mentioned 71. "Living well with others" was the category of behavior cited most often as "valued" by both parents and students. This category of "behavior" encompassed details such as

- "respecting others";
- "being kind";
- "courteous";
- "considerate";
- "friendly";
- "helpful";
- "polite";
- "concerned";
- "being able to work in a team";
- "volunteering";
- "being charitable."

"Demonstrating personal strengths" included indicators such as

- "being confident";
- "self-motivated";
- "enthusiastic";
- "assertive";

- "focused";
- "persevering";
- "responsible";
- "determined";
- "attentive";
- being "an independent thinker";
- being "proactive";
- "avoiding complacency";
- being "brave";
- having "initiative";
- being "self-disciplined";
- having "self-respect."

The category "working hard; discipline" captured behaviors such as

- being "able to maintain high grades";
- "following rules";
- "effective study habits";
- "setting goals";
- "prioritizing study";
- "doing homework";
- "covering necessary work even when ill";
- "listening to teachers";
- "being productive";
- "craving for success";
- "taking pride in one's work."

Whereas the above three categories were the responses most frequently expressed by parents and students, "participating in school activities" and "practicing good morals" were mentioned fairly frequently by parents and students. Responses that were shared infrequently, even only once, are considered to be significant in a study such as this, bearing in mind that the question was open-ended and that the subjective views of each participant who is a major stakeholder in the school ought to be considered. The following behaviors (though some are expressed as abilities), therefore, are presented as being important to only one or a few parents or students:

- being able to organize activities;
- being loyal to school;
- being able to converse intelligently;

- healthy habits;
- good attendance and punctuality;
- being religious/spiritual;
- etiquette;
- continuing what they learnt at school;
- mixing academic and fun;
- demonstrating good citizenship;
- common sense.

Parents' and students' advice for creating and maintaining "excellence" in students at the school

Parents' advice fell under six main categories and students' advice was divided among five categories as presented below.

Teacher attitudes and strategies

The majority of parent and student comments had to do with teacher attitudes and strategies. Parents' advice in this category included

- "teachers should help students to understand class work";
- "should be more focused on developing teaching materials";
- "should be more innovative";
- "should involve students more in interactive dialogue";
- "should pay more attention to girls' projects that are being used for exams";
- school should "ensure that teachers are well-prepared and have a pre-planned lesson before classes";
- school should "give constructive criticism."

Students' advice on teaching strategies included

- "give us the work we are supposed to get";
- "have class prepared before you come to class";
- "test the work that was taught";
- "stick to the point";
- "answer all students' questions";
- "explain all work";
- "tell us in advance when we have tests";
- "give struggling student individual attention";
- "don't just Google and give notes."

Of note in this category is that in eight instances students commented that there should be more use of technology in their classrooms. In terms of teacher attitudes, parents' advice included that teachers

- "should not compare students";
- "should lead by example";
- "be mentors/role models";
- "not 'talk down' to students";
- must respect by "doing what is right and truthful";
- "must be patient and understanding knowing that students would make mistakes";
- "be firm without 'buffing'";
- "be on time to class";
- "have an open mind."

Students advised that teachers:

- "be fair";
- "have an open heart";
- "help us when we are in need";
- "encourage innovative thinking";
- "be more understanding";
- demonstrate "more consideration" and "caring";
- use "no bad/mean words";
- "trust us more";
- "be more approachable";
- engage in "counseling for troubled students rather than shouting/embarrassing/pushing them without knowing the depth of the situation";
- "don't make a scene";
- "try to listen to excuses";
- "respect students' rights."

Discipline

A relatively large number of comments were made about standards of discipline. Generally, parents felt that the school should "continue to enforce rules." Students' suggestions included the following: that the staff "enforce a stern form of discipline for all types of disrespect and ill-mannered nonsense"; "develop a committee to deal with disrespectful students"; "develop a program to keep students 'at bay' instead of having them free and sitting like rubbish all over the place"; "organize disciplinary sessions to help students understand their functions/rules/responsibilities as a student"; that teachers or the school administration exercise punitive measures to enforce rules, to monitor students to keep them alert, and to "continue to remind them of the rules."

What students should learn

Three parents expressed the view that students should learn about "good morals and values," five felt that students needed to learn about proper etiquette, three suggested counseling for students, two were of the view that they should be prepared to "carry the behaviors and attitudes learnt in school into their adult life." Other comments were that they should know "how to accept and laugh at one's own shortcomings," learn "racial and cultural tolerance," and that home economics should be implemented "to develop all rounded women of the future who can be able to take care of a family."

Enabling a sense of belonging

Only parents made comments in this category. Among seven parents there were those who felt that parents should either have more access to teachers, have more collaboration with teachers, or that the school should "display positive behaviors to parents first, then to students." One parent felt that students should not be forced "to participate in religious activities," another, that the school should "allow freedom of expression to be individuals," and one other thought that there should be "consultation with students in matters that affect the school functioning smoothly."

In 19 instances, parents felt that there was no need for improvement in terms of preparing the students to have excellent behavior and attitudes, and in the case of students, four of them felt no advice was necessary.

Discussion and conclusion

It is evident that at this school, culture is conceptualized in ways similar to Peterson (2008), Hoyle (1986), and Owens (1987). There was the view that traditions were a significant part of the culture as well as the general atmosphere, a synonym for "ethos". Values and perpetuation of the school spirit and customs were also deemed important. It was felt that the rules were not enough to create a culture but appropriate behavior and "just knowing it" were crucial. These views echo Peterson's explanation of school culture as inclusive of "cherished traditions, unwritten rules, unspoken expectations, a proud heritage or past, and a sense of spirit." The "hidden curriculum" referred to by Owens (1987) is what teachers are finding hard to deliver. Teachers are recognizing that it is difficult to devise "mechanisms" for creating "spirit" and "propriety" in students. The irony emerges, however, when the data show that although "discipline" was cited by 29% of the students, and "attitude and behavior of the girls" was seen by ten students as main reasons the school is considered a first choice school, there were several instances where a few students either did not agree with specific school rules, or only some of the time were polite to others, were diligent, or saw themselves as role models, or where some of the time many and not all of them sang their school hymn with pride, related well to others or appreciated their school.

At the same time, "shared values", which is so much a component of school culture according to CEP (Character Education Partnership) as cited by Lickona et al. (1995) and Peterson (2008), may be the issue which is causing the concern for some of the teachers at the school. The responses from both parents and students indicate that there is a fair amount of disagreement with rules, and evidence that behaviors and attitudes that are considered desirable by the school are not always valued by all parents and are not always practiced or demonstrated by all students. Thus, the divide between school expectations and parent and student opinion is a cause for dialogue to enable dissection of the issues according to Kohn (1997).

However, there do exist certain traditions of the school which contribute to a large extent to the overall climate of the school and which were cited as being especially valued by both parents and students. The traditions valued were the ones where the school community, either parents, teachers and students, or teachers and students, shared the same space and collaborated in the same activity which required less formality than regular "school life". Perhaps it is in these settings that the conventional norms of "good" behavior (Purpel, 1991) and the moral niceties and social tranquility (Lockwood, 1991) could be dispensed with momentarily, giving the community the opportunity to be more human and less rigid.

All of this is not to say that the school is the enemy. The data do show that to a large extent, there is general consensus on many aspects that contribute to the school culture envisioned by this institution. However, if this culture is perceived at a superficial level, and even if it is viewed at a deeper level, it may indeed be challenging for faculty to overcome the "tidal waves" of social change to which Deal (1990) refers. Indeed, it is that challenge that prompted this research in the first place. It may be that the changes that are being perceived in the climate and culture of this school call for more communication and collaboration among the major stakeholders within this school community (Fong, 2006), not to mention professional preparation for school administrators and teaching staff to enable them to analyze and recreate as necessary their philosophy and how that is translated in the new vision of school community.

References

Berger, R. (2003). *An Ethic of Excellence: Building a Culture of Craftsmanship With Students.* Plymouth, NH: Heinemann.

Character Education Partnership (CEP) (2010). *Developing and Assessing School Culture—A New Level of Accountability for Schools—A Position Paper of the Character Education Partnership (CEP).* HYPERLINK "http://www.character.org" www.character.org

Conor, P.E. & Lake, L.K. (1988). *Managing Organisational Change.* New York. Praeger.

Deal, T. E. (1993). The culture of schools. In M. Shaskin & H. J. Walberg (Eds), *Educational Leadership and School Culture* (pp. 3–18). Berkeley, CA: McCutchan Publishing Company.

De Charms, R. (1983). *Personal Causation: The Internal Affective Determinants of Behavior.* Hillsdale, NJ: Erlbaum.

Elbot, C.F. & Fulton, D. (2008). *Building an Intentional School Culture: Excellence in Academics and Character.* Thousand Oaks, CA: Corwin Press.

Finnan, C. (2000). "Implementing school reform models: Why is it so hard for some schools and easy for others?" Paper presented at the meeting of the American Educational Research Association, New Orleans, April 2000.

Fong, K. I. S. (2006). Complexity theory and staff development. Paper presented at the Asia-Pacific Educational Research Association International Conference, November, 2006. Hong Kong: Hong Kong Institute of Education.

Hardy, L. (2003). Overburdened, overwhelmed. *American School Board Journal, 190*(4), 18–23.

Hinde. E. R. (2004). School culture and change: an examination of the effects of school culture on the process of change. http://usca.edu/essays/vol122004/hinde.pdf. Retrieved January 26, 2011.

Hoyle, E. (1986). *The Politics of School Management*. London: Hodder and Stoughton.

Kilpatrick, W. (1992). *Why Johnny Can't Tell Right from Wrong*. New York: Simon & Shuster.

Kohn, A. (1997). How not to look at character education. *Phi Delta Kappan*. February.

Leithwood, K., Leonard, L. & Sharratt, L. (1998). Conditions fostering organizational learning in school. *Educational Administration Quarterly*, 34, 2, 243–276.

Lickona, L. Schaps, E., & Lewis, C. (1995). *Eleven Principles of Effective Character Education* Washington, DC: Character Education Partnership.

Lockwood, A. L. (1991). Character education: the ten percent solution. *Social Education*, April/May, 246–248.

Lumby, J. & Foskett, N. (2011). Power, risk, and utility: interpreting the landscape of culture in educational leadership. *Educational Administration Quarterly*, 47, 3, 446–461.

Owens, R. (1987). *Organizational Behavior in Education* (3rd edn). New Jersey: Prentice-Hall.

Peterson, K. D. (2008). Excerpts from an interview with Dr. Kent Peterson in *School Culture. Shaping School Culture*. Apple Learning Exchange. http://ali.apple.com/ali_sites/ali/exhibits/1000488/. Retrieved January 26, 2011.

Purpel, D. E. (1991). Moral Education: an idea whose time has gone. *The Clearing House*, 64, 5, 309–312.

Sarason, S. (1996). *Re visiting "the culture of the school and the problem of change."* New York: Teachers College Press.

Silins, H., Zarins, S., & Mulford, B. (2002). What characteristics and processes define a school as a learning organisation? Is this a useful concept to apply to schools? *International Education Journal*, 3, 1, 24–32.

Yin, R. (1994). *Case Study Research: Design and Methods* (2nd edn). Thousand Oaks, CA: Sage Publishing.

3
A Study of Student Stress at the Senior Level at an All Girls Secondary School—A Case Study

Abstract: *This study examined stress in senior students at a high achieving all girls school (School T) in Trinidad and Tobago. Separate focus group interviews with students and teachers guided the questionnaire administered to 63 final year students of the school. Closed and open-ended questions were used. Data were analyzed both quantitatively with descriptive statistics, and qualitatively to highlight the students' voices. The findings show that whereas some students are able to manage their home and school commitments, the majority found a combination of school and home to be the cause of their stress. Most students speak with girlfriends, pray, and listen to music to cope with their stress. Many suggestions were offered to the school, and to family for easing their stress.*

Yamin-Ali, Jennifer. *Data-Driven Decision-Making in Schools: Lessons from Trinidad.* New York: Palgrave Macmillan, 2014. DOI: 10.1057/9781137412393.0007.

Introduction and background

Student stress is undeniably a concern for all educators especially as it sometimes culminates without prior manifestation to the unsuspecting observer. Much of the research done on human stress is logically approached from either a psychological, psycho-social, or bio-psychological standpoint. Human stress is directly related to the mind, the body and in many cases, the environment. Chronic stress in adults has received much attention in the medical field and recently, according to Little Flower et al. (2011), it is proposed that stress research should involve environmental factors and individual processes of perception and coping with stress. The interest that Little Flower et al. (2011) had in chronic stress and its resultant physical outcomes in adults led them to conduct their research on stress in adolescent students, with the belief that early intervention may bring about impactful corrective measures.

This study is situated in a social context where historically, education has been a key contributory factor in social mobility. The setting is post-colonial and post-Independence Trinidad where prior to Independence in 1962, the mainstream Christian Churches, through education and the establishment of schools, sought to evangelize the slaves, ex-slaves, and indentured workers. There eventually ensued a competition for government subventions for running schools with the introduction of a dual provision in education—government and Church. The Churches eventually gained governmental financial support. Citizens, up to this time, have the right to select which school they attend, and especially in the secondary sector, there is much competition for places. Since education is seen by most of the population to be the major determinant of their "success", there is rife competition to attend what are perceived to be the best schools.

The school under study is considered a "first choice school" in Trinidad due to its track record of high academic achievement and students' involvement in extra and co-curricular activities. "First choice" is determined by the number of students selecting it as their first choice of placement in the Secondary Entrance Assessment (SEA). It was established in 1912 by missionaries whose standards and values, through the school's continued affiliation with the local Church, still undergird the school's mission. The school places a high value on its traditions and and is supported by a vibrant network of alumnae. The religious quality of the school is maintained by the legal appointment of senior school administrators who are practicing members of the local Church.

It is in this context that students function. The school sets high standards and is itself in competition with other schools for national scholarships and the public's approval. Parents, having in many cases made great personal sacrifices to ensure that their daughters excel in the SEA to gain entry in the school, have high expectations of them.

It is not unexpected that teachers would also be affected by these high levels of expectations of both students and their parents. This study of student stress came about through the concerns of three teachers who were randomly approached to discuss an area of school life which they felt needed some sort of analysis and possible intervention. They all agreed that student stress at the Form Six level (final two years of secondary school) was a great concern to them. Thus, with their support, this study was elaborated.

Adolescent stress has received much attention from researchers in education (Hardy, 2003; Pope, 2001; Torsheim & Wold, 2001) and from others (Muuss, 2006; Cobain, 1998; Slaby & Garfinkel, 1994; Colten & Gore, 1991; Hall, 1904). The causes of this stress vary and students' ability to cope with their stress may depend on their inner resources or the support they have in their environment.

In G. S. Hall's (1904) seminal work on adolescent stress, he coined the phrase "storm and stress" to capture this adolescent experience. His treatment of "storm and stress" considers that the stress experience and coping with it will vary according to individual and cultural background. It is recognized that adolescent storm and stress tend to be lower in traditional cultures than in the West but may increase as globalization increases individualism.

Because Trinidadian society, in its plurality, comprises second and third generation descendants of primary Eastern cultures and the continental African culture, it can be found that cultural traits combined with the social realities of post-colonialism, such as the zeal to achieve, "get ahead" and compete, emerge as determinants of patterns of behavior in the student population, especially as they recognize that education is a major key to opening the proverbial door to success.

Views of adolescent stress will determine how one addresses it. The popular views or "myths" may cloud the ability or the necessity to provide the appropriate support for the stressed. According to Arnett (2007), research has refuted many myths about adolescent stress, but he points out that related myths have sprouted in recent times around emerging adulthood. He highlights three of those myths as being that a) they suffer from a normative "crisis," b) they are "selfish," c) they are reluctant to "grow up" and become adults. His research shows that that these myths exaggerate or falsify the true experience of emerging adults.

Since this study focuses on stress among adolescent students, the following studies shed further light on stress in the context of students and in a variety of contexts which may be relevant to this research context.

Torsheim and Wold (2001) examined the relationship between school-related stress, social support from teachers and classmates, and somatic complaints in the general population of Norwegian adolescents. Analysis from self-reports from a representative sample of 4,952 Norwegian 11- to 15-year-olds revealed that students with high levels of school-related stress had a higher odds ratio (OR) for weekly headache (4.1), abdominal pain (3.9), backache (4.8), dizziness (5.4), and coexisting somatic complaints (6.1). It was found that students with low classmate support had a consistently higher OR for weekly symptoms. There was no significant relationship between school-related stress and social support. Findings suggest that adolescents' frequency of somatic complaints may reflect partly their ability to adapt to ordinary school demands.

The issue of social support becomes tinged with irony in a context where the student's social milieu creates the stress factors. For example, in a study conducted by Einstein, Lovibond, and Gaston (2000) which examined the relationship between *perfectionism* and emotional symptoms, final-year high school students in Australia completed the Multidimensional Perfectionism scale and the Depression Anxiety and Stress Scales (DASS) 10 weeks (n = 673) and again 10 days (n = 505) before a major set of examinations. Elevated symptoms of depression, anxiety, and stress were evident on both test occasions. More than 20% of the sample fell into the severe range. When perfectionism was self-driven it was not strongly related to emotional symptoms. On the other hand, when it was socially driven it was positively related to depression and anxiety. Students whose parents were born overseas (outside of Australia) reported higher levels of socially prescribed perfectionism, and higher levels of depression and anxiety. The findings of this study were interpreted within Higgins' (1987) self-discrepancy theory, which makes a link between high externally imposed standards and emotional distress. The results suggest that adolescents who perceive strong external pressure to excel academically are at risk of severe emotional symptoms under examination stress.

A study based on adolescent students in Chandigarh, India (Arun & Chavan, 2009) collected data from 2402 students (mixed gender) and concluded that students with academic problems and an unsupportive environment at home perceived life as a burden and had higher rates of suicidal ideations. One-half of those students found study and related issues as problems. Academic decline significantly correlated with the feeling of "life as a burden" and suicidal ideations. Of all the students 38.4% identified future planning as a source of their problems. Future planning included choice of subject, college, career, lack of clarity, and confidence about such planning. Also significant was the positive correlation between relationship with peers and parents and psychological health. One-fourth of the students identified problem issues such as frequent arguments among parents, criticizing and interfering attitudes of parents, disagreements between student and parent, poor trust, high expectations, and lack of guidance. Changes in living conditions, in the health of a family member and in financial status of parents were shown to be significantly stressful events in 40%–70% of the students studied by Little Flower et al. (2011) in Hyderabad, India.

In a study of stress among college students in Taiwan, Kai-Wen (2009) noted, from responses gathered from 201 students, that the strongest stressors for the students were lack of sleep, being inferior to others, lack of concentration, physical appearance, lack of family support, getting along with siblings, parents' excessively high expectations, lack of interest in certain subjects, having trouble getting along with peers, and considering life and their own future. In this research, difference between the genders emerged showing that male students were more stressed by family factors than were female students.

It is interesting to note that research conducted by the U.S. Department of Education in 2005 found that whereas single-sex schools rated higher in school achievement, in co-educational schools self-esteem in students was higher than in students of single-sex schools and offered a friendlier and more relaxed atmosphere with more opportunities for pleasure-centered social contact.[1] This has implications for levels of school stress as it relates to school context and perhaps even coping with stress.

Coping with stress in adolescent students is an area addressed by many institutions either in the form of research or implementation of programs to help students. However, the coping strategies that individuals opt to use can impact their experience of the stress. Gibson (2004) noted that some persons use behavioral and emotional avoidance to avoid thinking or having feelings about their stress. This is important for teachers to understand since such behavior can easily mask a student's need for help. Other researchers have shown that engaging in avoidance-type coping may result in more severe psychological symptoms (Hayes, Wilson, Gifford, Follette, & Strosahl, 1996; Spira, Zvlensky, Eifert, & Feldner, 2004; Ramya & Parthasarathy, 2009) than dealing with the facts related to the stress.

Teaching adolescents life-skills was an intervention studied by Srikata and Kumar (2010) in the context of a one-year trial with 605 adolescents with similar demographic backgrounds from two secondary schools. Their findings indicate that the students in the program had significantly better self-esteem, adequate coping, and adjustment capability. They describe Life Skills Education (LSE) as a program that teaches generic life skills using games, debates, role-plays, and group discussion. They advise that these skills be practiced in a non-threatening setting. Access to this practice provides the adolescent with a wide range of alternative and creative ways of solving problems in real life.

Pitzer (1985) and Walker (2002), in publications coming out of the University of Minnesota, both suggest that young people need to learn and practice coping skills to cope with conflict or with a problem. Self-responsibility should characterize coping strategies which seek relief through positive, non-destructive ways. They also stress communication skills, including the ability to select a good listener. Students should be actively taught problem-solving skills as well as how to sort out issues, set goals, and make plans for the future.

The latter findings indicate that casual advice and simply organizing oneself may not be sufficient for students whose stress is unmanageable. Students who simply cannot cope with their level of stress sometimes resort to the ultimate defeat—suicide.

In one study (Brunner et al., 2007), it was found that academic problems were associated with deliberate self-harm and another study (Logaraj, Felix, & Vedapriya 2005) associated such problems with more stress. Lalwani, Sharma, Kabra, Girdhar, and Dogra (2004) reported that the months of March to July are when examination results are announced and when entrance into college and the beginning of the new academic year are upon students. They made an association between these factors and student suicide. Guar, Murthy, and Nathawat (2001) and Latha and Reddy (2006) reported that 56% of student suicides in Delhi occurred in these months. The suicide factor is relevant to any deliberation on human stress including that of adolescent students.

When students are unable to cope with school-related stress coupled with other stress, schools must necessarily look for ways in which stress can be reduced or ways in which stressed students can be helped. Pope and Simon (2005) suggest a variety of strategies which schools may utilize to minimize students' stress. They note that high achievers "do everything and do it well." They are involved in a wide range of activities including community service and school leadership. Yet, all that activity is summed up as "doing school" where the learning and the enjoyment are not necessarily meaningful but a means to an end: "to get good grades, which brings them to college, which brings them the high-paying job, which brings them to happiness, so they think" (Pope, 2001:4). An initiative at the Wheatley School, a public high school in the affluent community of Old Westbury, New York, saw the school giving copies of *Doing School* (Pope, 2001) to each faculty member and all interested students and parents. Time was allotted during the school day for extensive discussion and debate about student stress. In a short space of time, a commitment was made to reducing student stress at school and an action plan was developed by all major stakeholders. The school has implemented that plan. In addition, teachers have begun to announce homework assignments well in advance, reduce the amount of homework they give (especially on weekends), and offer more extra-credit opportunities. Teachers are more generous about testing, while the school community has suggested giving more long-term, meaningful assignments, such as unit projects that focus on mastery of skills; making vacation homework-free; teaching students ways to relax in stressful situations; and educating parents about the effects of stress and pressure. Though the effects of these strategies would have been seen in the long-term, the immediate result was that teachers say the problem is real and feel more empathy toward the students.

Partly inspired by the Wheatley project, the advisory board at Stanford University responded to nationwide reports of increased anxiety and depression among college students (Benton, Robertson, Tseng, Newton, & Benton 2003). The response was the creation of an intervention named "Stressed Out Students" (SOS) project where dialogue with the public and ongoing team work between 15 schools resulted in specific guidelines to reduce student stress.

Even as Pope and Simon (2005) applaud the Wheatley and Stanford initiatives, they recognize that it won't be easy to change the culture in school and society that places a premium on academic achievement and competition. They suggest that colleges and universities need to come on board and send different messages to high school students. They report that some, like Stanford and MIT, have made changes in their admissions practices. One example is that MIT now limits the number of extra-curricular activities a candidate may list on the application and asks students to write an essay about what gets them excited.

Methodology

This research employed a descriptive case study approach. It is a single case which features both qualitative and quantitative methodologies. It follows the description of case study research by Yin (1994) which indicates that the focus of case study research is on a contemporary phenomenon within its real-life context where boundaries between the phenomenon and its context are not clearly evident. Yin also points out that this approach is suitable for studying complex social phenomena—in the case of this study, the phenomenon of student stress in a particular real context.

This study uses an embedded design within the case study paradigm. The analysis sought consistent patterns of evidence across units within the single case.

The questions guiding the study were:

- To what extent do Form Six students of School T (pseudonym) experience stress?
- What are the sources of stress that these Form Six students face?
- How do these Form Six students deal with stress?
- What recommendations do these students make with regard to the sources of stress that they face?

For the purposes of this research, "stress" was specified as "school-related", "home-related", and "other".

The school under study is an all-girls secondary school which is church affiliated but financed largely by the government. It has a tradition of conservative values and practices as well as a record of high overall achievement. It is associated with high standards in all its endeavors including extra and co-curricular activities. The senior level of the school comprises two years—Lower Six and Upper Six.

Data collection was initiated when the researcher was trying to establish a culture of data-driven decision-making at the school. She interviewed a three-member team of teachers from the school to ascertain any major area of concern they had with regard to any aspect of school life in their context. The three teachers agreed that the stress level of students in the senior years (Forms Lower and Upper Six) was a major concern for them. This concern translated into the need to find out from students to what extent they experienced stress, what the sources of stress were, how they coped with their stress, and what were their recommendations.

The researcher then developed a research plan with the team, elaborated the data collection instruments and shared it with the team for their input. The team of three teachers between themselves conducted individual interviews with six random Form Upper Six students to glean some general information about the stress issue. These interviews were driven by a semi-structured guide, allowing for the interviewers to converse in a natural way based on the responses and comments being presented by the students. These interviews were transcribed and the content was used to develop a questionnaire for the target group for Upper Six students (N-105).

A member of the three-teacher team also conducted a semi-structured focus group interview with a group of six Form Six teachers to get their perceptions of Form Six student stress. The group sample was purposive in that teachers from different subject areas were preferred for wider representation. This interview was transcribed and the responses fed into the student questionnaire for the accessible sample of 63. The researcher's understanding of the context also contributed to the content of the questionnaire.

The questionnaire was first administered to a pilot sample of ten random students from the entire UVI class. The pilot allowed for review and minor amendments before administering to a convenience sample of 63 students who were available at the time. All students filled out the questionnaires anonymously. This was because the information being sought was of a highly personal nature.

The questionnaire consisted of nine closed-ended questions and six open-ended questions. The open-ended questions sought students' elaboration on choices made in the closed-ended questions as well as their suggestions.

Analysis was done on a quantitative basis for the closed-ended questions. Patterns and trends were sought through that analysis as well. Cross analysis allowed for deeper insights into phenomena and individuals within the sample. For the open-ended questions, recurring themes were recognized and categorized. Deeper analysis was made possible through comparison of responses within groups and across groups.

Findings are presented below according to the research questions.

Findings

General sources of stress

The largest number of students found a large amount of stress (varying from 7–10 on a scale of 1–10) to be brought about by home plus school (24/63). Generally, home plus school were the causes identified for most of the stress experienced by students. It is also significant that five students found that friends were the reason for their relatively high level of stress. Schoolwork only, without other causes was a source of stress to varying degrees.

School-related stress

Causes and extent of students' school-related stress

Ranking highest as a cause of *fair to great stress* for most students were

- their own pressure to excel (94%);
- amount of homework (90%);
- having to do additional things in addition to regular school work e.g., extra-curricular activities and chores (90%);
- their own high standards (89%);
- their own pressure to get a scholarship (81%);
- pressure from their teachers to perform well (77%);
- too much homework to cover today for tomorrow (77%).

It is worth noting that not having enough time to complete their school obligations like homework and extra-curricular duties, plus chores at home, accounts for the stress that most of the students face. Time is also indicated as a major stress factor since 77% of the students feel that not enough time is given to complete assignments.

Students experiencing stress from interrelated factors

There were three factors related to high performance that were selected as causing *a lot of* or *great stress* by the same 26 individuals. These students all experienced much stress because of:

- their own pressure to excel;
- their own pressure to get a scholarship; and
- their own high standards.

The number 26 is significant since the average number of national scholarships won by senior students at the school in the last academic year was 29. These students, in this context, may view their stress as positive in the sense that it is goal oriented.

There were two factors related to homework which were selected by the same 21 students as causing them high stress. These were:

- teachers not understanding that you did not have time or did not understand (re homework); and
- teachers giving excessive homework and not correcting it.

These two factors have implications for justified student frustration, and also for teachers' sense of responsibility in terms of pedagogy.

Related to the above issue of pedagogy is the finding that nine students all selected the following two factors as causing them much stress:

- teachers giving excessive homework and not correcting it; and
- when they don't understand some areas of the syllabus.

There is reason to question whether the lack of homework correction with its consequent feedback has a direct relation to students' lack of understanding of the syllabus. However, this question cannot be answered by these data but it raises an issue for further investigation.

On a more subjective note, 12 students all experienced much stress because they were concerned about:

- teachers'/principal's impression of them; and
- having to keep up the "appearance" of coping.

These two items can be particularly stressful since they are outside of the control of the students and would place students in a position where their energies are focused on others rather than constructively on their own performance and overall growth.

At least one half of the respondents are stressed *a lot* or *to a great extent* by the following:

- their own pressure to excel;
- their own high standards;
- having to do additional things in addition to regular school work. (e.g. extra-curricular; chores);
- teachers not understanding that they did not have time or did not understand (re homework);
- their own pressure to get a scholarship;
- too much homework to cover today for tomorrow.

However, there are smaller but significant pockets of students who are stressed *a lot* or *to a great* extent by the following:

- teachers giving excessive homework and not correcting it;
- pressure from their teachers to perform well;
- when they do not understand some areas of the syllabus;
- completing university/college applications;
- teachers not recognizing their effort.

The smallest number experiencing a lot of or a great amount of stress for any single reason is 16/62 which is significant. Such a number *can* constitute a whole class in certain subject areas at the Form Six level, though this data does not indicate that the numbers reflect any single class.

Out of all the sources delineated above which cause significant stress to Form Six students, three sources are "self-inflicted". That is, an average of 62% of students see themselves, among other things, as the sources of their own stress. Those students stress themselves out due to:

- their own pressure to excel;
- their own high standards;
- their own pressure to get a scholarship.

Factors causing little or no stress at school

Yet, there are some students who said that they experience hardly any or no stress from school. The factors causing little or no stress to approximately 50 to 61% of the students are

- completing university/college applications (50%);
- pressure to measure up to their peers (55%);

- the irresponsibility of some of their peers (58%);
- teachers'/principal's impression of them (61%).

Those students offering reasons for little or no stress at school are quoted below:

- "An understanding of life";
- "Friends, family, God, lessons teacher";
- "Taking on a realistic amount of work (but stressed only when goals are not accomplished)";
- "Talking to close people; reorganizing myself";
- "I hardly do homework unless it is really important";
- "I am superior to the system."

Conflicting responses to certain stress factors

Interestingly, there were relatively comparative numbers of students responding in conflicting ways to the same stress factors as seen in Figure 3.1.

What stands out in the factors above is that none of them has to do with amount of school work or homework per se. Reaction to these factors may stem from their level of importance to the individual. Generally,

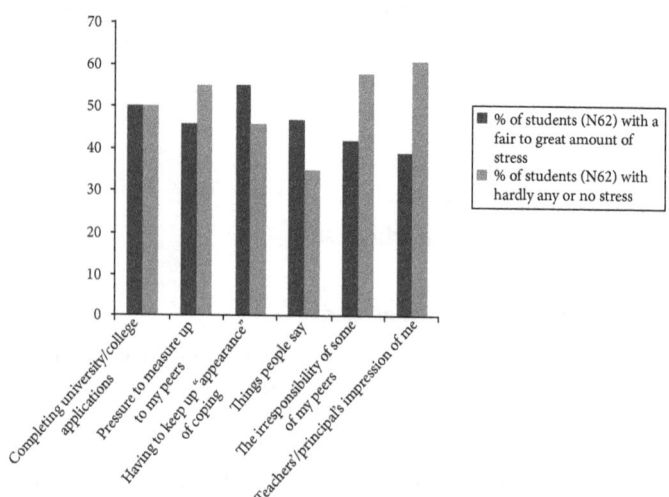

FIGURE 3.1 *Comparison of percentage of students with varying levels of stress*

Study of Student Stress 69

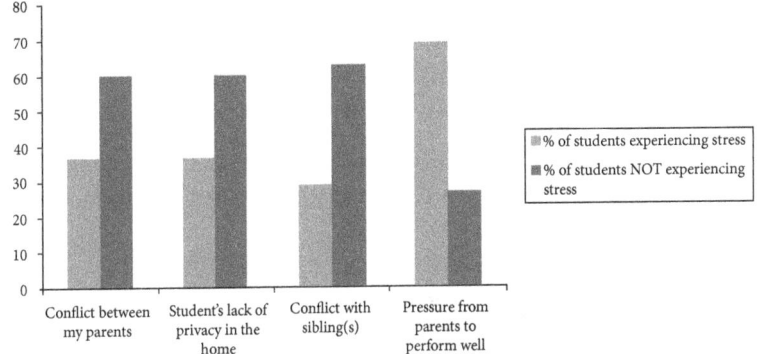

FIGURE 3.2   *Conflicting experiences of home-related stress*

these causes of stress relate to perspectives on life, relationships and how one views oneself in relation to others.

Home-related stress

Whereas only one student experienced stress from home only, 40 experienced varying levels of stress from a combination of home and school factors. However, there were also instances where significantly more students experienced little or no stress caused by certain factors as seen in Figure 3.2.

The contrast between the proportion of students who face a fair to great amount of stress from parents' pressure to perform well and those who don't is stark. It is the one area that shows the greatest amount of home-related stress experienced by the greatest percentage of students. This compares with the lower 27% who experience hardly any stress or no stress for this reason. Pressure to help with chores immediately had a somewhat balanced response from students in that 52% felt stressed by this, and 47% felt little or no stress due to this factor.

When compared to the percentages of students experiencing school-related stress, students experiencing home-related stress are fewer, though significant. The higher percentages of students experiencing school-related stress ranged from 77% to 94%, whereas the highest percentages of students experiencing home-related stress ranged from 37% to 69%. In terms of an issue such as student stress though, the source of stress and the number of students become less important than the realization that any one student is, in fact, experiencing stress. The danger lies in the lack of ability to cope with that stress.

Of those 21 students who chose to explain why they felt hardly or no stress at home, 16 gave the reason as family "support" or "understanding"—either "family," "parents," "mom," "single parent" or "grandmother." Other explanations offered were:

- "I prefer to ignore this stress—less important than school stress."
- "parents do not argue about serious affairs—hardly at home so I have privacy."
- "I create a comfortable environment for myself. I create circumstances which are positive and keep me happy."
- "(Close family unit) and friends who are *always* there for me."
- "Logic reigns supreme" (in her family).

The range of experiences and reactions to them makes for a dynamic psychological storm in and out of the classroom which teachers must be equipped to manage. Teachers and school administrators need to always be aware that whereas home may be a great source of support for some students, for others it is a source of stress.

Stress caused by other factors

The "other" factors that caused a fair to great amount of stress to the following percentages of students are:

- worrying about their future personal life (89%);
- worrying about not satisfying the academic expectations of their parent(s) (77%);
- too much time needed for extra-curricular activities (60%);
- wanting to excel at an extra-curricular activity (58%).

These sources of stress do reflect the highest ranking sources of school stress which had to do with excelling at school, time to allocate to extra-curricular activities or excelling at one, and what they perceived in their school-related stress to be *their* own pressure to excel or to win a scholarship. What these variables seem to point to is that students' school life is closely linked to their personal life, since the latter will, to some degree, be determined by their academic achievements.

Although statistically it is tempting to focus on trends and large percentages, in a small target population of approximately 100, and with a sample size of 62, the factors which caused "other" stress to 19%–58% of the sample are worthy of attention since those numbers range, out of a total of 62 students, between 12 and 36. These figures and factors are significant in terms of help that students may need that is non-academic. Recognizing that the following are acknowledged as stressful by any number of students, in addition to other sources of stress, may be useful for the school's administration and teachers:

- getting to and from school (39%);
- the health condition of a family member (37%);
- financial difficulty (32%);
- insufficient resources for supporting my school work (24%);
- relationship with a boyfriend (9%).

Isolated single cases included also:

- worrying about my friends;
- worrying about my dog;
- my health condition (two students);
- alcoholism in a close family member;
- religious struggles;
- absence of a mother;
- expectations from family.

Dealing with stress

Selecting from 24 items, the following is an indication of how students say they deal with school-related stress, home-related stress, and other stress.

More than 75% of the students cope with their school-related stress in three ways as shown in Figure 3.3.

Between 50% and 74% of them cope by:

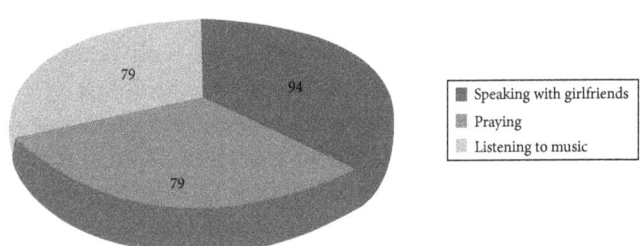

FIGURE 3.3 *Most common ways of coping with school-related stress*

- sleeping;
- trying not to take it on;
- preferring not to overburden other people with their worries and keep it to themselves and dealing with it;
- dancing;
- eating more;
- playing a sport;
- taking it out on someone else;
- meditating;
- going out;
- channeling their thoughts through writing;
- speaking with their boyfriend;
- speaking with their teachers;
- re-assessing and reorganizing themselves;
- thinking about the big picture.

Less common ways of coping included the following: Two to four students indicated that their coping mechanism was using alcohol, having suicidal thoughts or using medication. Seven students indicated that they did not have a coping mechanism.

Ways of coping with home-related stress

The most common way of dealing with home-related stress, as indicated by the students, is speaking with their girlfriends. Approximately two-thirds of the students deal with home-related stress by either praying, trying not to take it on, listening to music, or sleeping. About half of them resort to speaking with their parents, to their boyfriend, or thinking about the big picture. Up to two of them use medication or have suicidal thoughts and five of them do not have a coping mechanism.

Ways of coping with other-related stress

Over three-fourths of the student sample cope with other kinds of stress by speaking with girlfriends, whereas two-thirds cope by either praying, listening to music, trying not to take it on, or sleeping. Half of them speak with their parents, about one-third of them speak with their boyfriend or think about the big picture. Only five of them speak with the teachers about stress of this nature, one uses alcohol, one uses medication, and one has suicidal thoughts. Four of them do not have a coping mechanism for this type of stress.

In terms of patterns that warrant concern, it is the same student (T) who indicated that her way of dealing with school stress was by using medication and having suicidal thoughts, that her way of dealing with home-related stress was by using medication, and for other-related stress, by using medication and having suicidal thoughts. This is certainly a case for urgent intervention.

Student V coped with school and "other" stress by using alcohol and with home-related stress by using medication.

There were two students in all (O & V) who indicated that they used alcohol to deal with some form of stress, while there were four in all (AH, V, T, L) who relied on medication, and four (T, S, Q, H) who had thoughts of suicide from some form of stress. This exemplifies where small numbers in data can account for great concern depending on the context.

Students' recommendations to the principal and/or teachers

Students did suggest ways in which the principal or teachers could help to ease their stress. Figure 3.4 shows that their many suggestions covered a range of categories: homework/assignments/exams, quality of teaching, teacher attitudes, emotional needs, de-emphasizing academics, and organizational issues.

Of the seven most common suggestions made by students, four were related to homework, assignments, or exams. The others fell under quality of teaching, teacher attitudes, and de-emphasizing academics.

Table 3.1 lists the other suggestions made indicating in brackets the number of students making the suggestion:

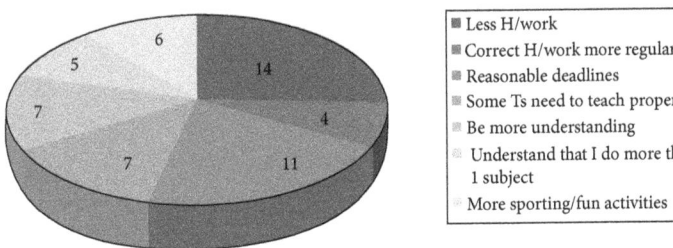

FIGURE 3.4   *Most common student suggestions*

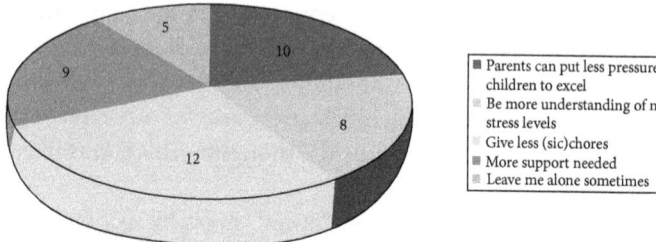

FIGURE 3.5   Students' suggestions for easing stress at home

TABLE 3.1   Students' suggestions

Homework/Assignments/Exams	Teacher attitudes
Ts should try and improve the kind of homework (2)	Appreciate Ss' efforts (1)
To should spend more time discussing vs. giving homework (1)	Understand that Ss do not always have time (a)
Be more understanding with h/wk or exams (1)	Ts should stop belittling Ss when they do not complete the work. Sometimes situations are beyond control (2)
Stop giving projects – no time (2)	Be less constricting, repressive (1)
Help a little more with assignments due (1)	Do not judge people at face value (1)
Correct h/wk more regularly (4)	Reward honesty and confession of issues (1)
Be more understanding when we are unable to complete h/wk for a valid reason (1)	Be more open-minded (2)
Explain EXACTLY what they want us to do – in terms of IA specifications (1)	Idolization of the 'smarter' individuals (1)
Ts should consult with each other when scheduling coursework (1)	Ts have an 'attitude' when I don't understand (1)
Quality of teaching	Do not victimize Ss (1)
Allow Ss to do anonymous evaluations of Ts (1)	Understand we're human … (1)
Some Ts are unsure of what they teach and tell us – Google it (1)	*Emotional needs*
More assistance with labs – seriously (1)	Individual meetings (1)
More fun activities in class (3)	Personal best (1)
Help Ss individually (1)	Back on track (1)
More worked examples (1)	Potential (1)
Staying on point during teaching (1)	Do not victimize Ss (1)
More assistance with lab books	Lessen expectations of Ss and understand that there is life other than school (1)
When we don't understand don't embarrass us by asking us to explain (1)	Have sessions allowing us to express our problems (1)

Continued

TABLE 3.1   *Continued*

Homework/Assignments/Exams	Teacher attitudes
Some Ts should not assume that all Ss learn at the same rate (1)	Have sessions to help us deal with stress (2)
Doing questions on topics before moving on may help (1)	*De-emphasizing academics*
Ts should consider ALL Ss not just bright ones (1)	Reduce emphasis on scholarships/pressure to excel (1)
Give breaks in class when a lot of work is being done (1)	Place less stress on the academic e.g. sanitizing school for hand and foot disease (1)
Ensure understanding before testing (1)	All the ceremonies – put pressure to excel (1)
Teacher attitudes	Less stress on scholarships (1)
Principal should try to motivate teachers because they take out their stress of meeting deadlines on students (1)	Incorporate classes like dance, music ... not for assessment (2)
Ts should not have a narrow-minded attitude and never lose their composure because of personal matters (1)	Allow Ss to bring iPods during lunch time (1)
Some Ts show favoritism (3)	*Organizational issues*
Be less abrasive with Ss (1)	Lacking (1)
Ts are harsh and unapproachable due to personal conflicts and affairs (1)	Better delegation of prefect duties (1)
Do not put unnecessary pressure on Ss – you do not know what is happening in their personal lives ... (1)	Have a counselor in school who can help with Univ [University] applications (2)
Try to be as gentle as possible – embarrassing Ss is not the way not go ... I HATE THAT! (Q) (1)	Give less (sic) school-related tasks e.g. prefect duties (3)

What is significant about these suggestions is that these students are saying that from their perspective, to some extent, these features are absent from their school experience.

As seen in Figure 3.5, there was some degree of commonality in some of the suggestions made for easing the stress at home, with the most common requesting fewer chores at home. Generally, clusters of students (5–10) wanted their parents to have a shift in their approach to dealing with them.

In more isolated cases a wide variety of suggestions were made with regard to the following six categories. All comments are direct quotations from the students.

Parents conducting their own lives

Relax a little; Go out sometimes; Be nicer; Argue less.

Parents' behavior

Talk as a family; Have family time; Sort out their issues without bringing them home; Stop taking out frustration on me; Learn to welcome conversation about uncomfortable topics; Talk to the child when they look as though they have trouble; Try not to get me into conflict between parents; Listen to me; When irritable do not get vex; Be easier to talk to; Do not burden me with financial problems; Do not chastise if I play music while I study—it relaxes and allows concentration; My mother can stop nagging me; My grandfather can stop drinking; Try to have a positive way of speaking to me rather than suppressing; Stop complaining about everything; Quarrel less.

Parents satisfying children's personal needs

Give more privacy for studying; Let me sleep in peace; Give me an hour for myself; Have more bonding sessions; Give me the space that I need and try to make my environment more study-friendly or appropriate.

Specific ways for parents to deal with children

Talk to you to find out how you are doing with school and life; Don't talk to me; Stop complaining about everything; Stop taking up stuff in my room; Stop questioning who I'm talking to on the phone; Reduce the small talk; Leave me alone when I'm doing work.

Parents' Attitudes and relationships

Have more confidence in us; Love; Parents should be aware that their daughters may want to have a career and NOT be a home-maker; Realize that stress at school is just as real as stress at work (maybe more intense); Be supportive of my personal choices; Be more supportive of my dreams/goals; Be open-minded if we share our problems; Be more understanding of my position as a member of the family and individual; Parents can understand that just because I'm home doesn't mean that I'm not busy.

Siblings

My siblings should be more supportive; Siblings can make less noise.

Students' suggestions about what others can do to ease their stress

Suggestions to people in general:
- People should be reasonable and logical.
- Be positive.
- Talk to me and give advice.
- Help me to relax.
- Be more patient.
- Listen more.
- Be more caring and supportive (five persons).
- Be less annoying.
- Stop comparing me to other people.
- Stop CRITICIZING.
- Think about what we need.
- People could give me my space to cope.
- A little leisure once in a while.
- Talk to us about our future expectations.
- Just be a good, understanding friend and offer assistance if you can.
- Be more understanding and open-minded.
- The gov't can help Ss financially.
- Help me to manage my time efficiently.
- I prefer to be left alone at times.
- Be there to hear me vent.
- Listen without judgment.
- Let me talk to an adult.
- Listen to my problems; be more friendly.
- Friends can listen and understand.
- Listen and provide advice.
- Cheer me up with laughter.
- Smile now and then.
- Ask how I'm going, if everything is okay.
- Talking and being there for me.
- Friends should make school fun and stress-free.
- Sharing their opinion and stories.
- Reassurance.
- Give me personal space.
- Don't be judgy or preachy to me.
- Listen; Don't pretend to listen.

- Do not give advice unless I ask you.
- Do not take it seriously if I snap at them for no reason.
- Try not to annoy the stressed person with insular thoughts and comments.
- Give hugs and show love.
- Liming [local phrase meaning "socializing"] with all my friends tends to calm me because their conversation distracts me and lightens my mood.
- Encouragement to excel.
- If you know we are dealing with specific problems do not demand too much of us.
- Allow me to express myself.
- My friends create a warm, carefree environment that only requires me to be there and relax, nothing else.
- Mutual support between my friends and me.

Suggestions for home

- Make allowance/money accessible in a timely manner without having to ask every month.
- Parents can be less demanding and try to understand.
- Organize life better.
- Buy me ice-cream.
- Help me financially.
- Breeze out time.
- My mother encourages me to do my homework and lets me stay home to do what I have to do to excel.
- Going out once in a while.
- Take me out of the house often.
- Sleep relaxes me.
- Going out allows me to clear my mind.
- Family and friends always being there for me.

Suggestions for school

- Those in charge of extra-curricular activities should realize that we're students first.
- Make community service less, or more fun.
- Less h/wk so I have more time for community service etc.

- Understand that after studying all day and night (at home), if we spend our free periods doing nothing it's not wasting time, but relaxing with a friend.
- More information—careers etc.
- Stress-relieving activities—yoga, dance.
- Guidance counseling.
- Train teachers to listen/care.
- Give me some time off.
- Talk to my parents.
- Assist with academic assignments.
- Let me use free periods to rest instead of helping teachers.
- My principal and Ts do not harass me for coming to school late often because they understand my situation.
- Playing cards.
- Teachers shouldn't criticize others and gossip.
- Give more holidays to do nothing—just relax.

Discussion and conclusion

Although the reputation of this particular school hinges on its extra-curricular activities as part of its effort to offer holistic development to its students, the demands that this places on students' time and energy seem to create a hidden systemic conflict.

The issue of excessive homework, not correcting homework, and the emphasis on planning and time-management for students raise the question of quantity versus quality which is an area to consider in teacher development planning for the school. It may be that there is too much of a focus on practice and "busy work" without sufficient emphasis on concept formation. The need for evaluating what teachers do and what teachers and parents expect as in the Wheatley School intervention (Pope & Simon, 2005) needs to be addressed.

Students' suggestions about what school could do to ease their stress point to a need for a whole school approach to possible improvement in the areas of "homework/assignments/exams," "quality of teaching," "teacher attitudes," "emotional needs," "de-emphasizing academics," and "organisational issues." In other words, student stress doesn't seem to be just a student issue, but a school issue as in the case of the Wheatley School cited earlier.

Underlying school stress, emerging from this study, is the adolescent need for "space" and "respect" as a person, as detailed in students' suggestions for how their stress at home could be eased. In any study of adolescent student stress, one must consider within the normal "storm and stress" of adolescence, the reality of the cultural background of students and how that may color the environment they live in and the way they respond to it (Hall, 1904). In addition, schools must not fall prey to accepting the myths about adolescent stress which cloud the true experience of these emerging adults (Arnett, 2007).

The way forward for this high-achieving school points to a need to harness a situation that is potentially spiraling out of control, bearing in mind that its administration and staff have undergone much turnover in very recent times. There seems to be a need to attend to developmental needs at the school organizational level, at the staff level, and at the student level. In addition to recommendations made above, at the student level, the efforts of Srikata and Kumar (2010) could be considered in order to develop a practical Life Skills program for students.

Attending to the findings of this study may be an initial step in the effort to meet the needs of the Form Six students of the school. Such an effort would surely fulfill a criterion within the school's vision which is "to deconstruct established ideals of learning and recreate a dynamic process of education which reforms and refashions itself according to individual needs and expectations."

Note

1 *Single-sex versus secondary schooling: a systematic review, Washington, D.C.: U.S. Department of Education. Office of Planning, Evaluation, Policy and Program Studies Service; 2005, p. 85.*

References

Arun, Priti & Chavan, B. S. (2009). Stress and suicidal ideas in adolescent students in Chandigarh. *Indian Journal of Medical Sciences*, 63, 7, 281–287.

Arnett, Jeffrey Jensen (1999). Adolescent storm and stress, reconsidered. *American Psychologist*, 54, 5, May, 317–326.

Arnett, Jensen Jeffrey (2007). Review paper: suffering, selfish, slackers? Myths and reality about emerging adults. *Journal of Youth and Adolescence, 36*, 1, 23–29.

Benton, S. A., Robertson, J. M., Tseng, W., Newton, F. B., & Benton, S. L. (2003). Changes in counseling center client problems across 13 years. *Professional Psychology: Research and Practice, 34*, 1, 66–72.

Brunner, R., Parzer, P., Haffner, J., Steen, R., Roos, J., Klett, M., & Resch, F. (2007). Prevalence and psychological correlates of occasional and repetitive deliberate self harm in adolescents. *Arch Pediatr Adolesc Med, 161*, 641–649.

Cobain, B. (1998). *When Nothing Matters Anymore: A Survival Guide for Depressed Teens*. Minnesota: Free Spirit Publishing, Inc., 1998.

Colten, E. M. & Gore, S. (Eds.) (1991). *Adolescent Stress: Causes and Consequences*. New York: Aldine de Gruyter.

Einstein, D. A., Lovibond, P. F. & Gaston, J. E. (2000). Relationship between Perfectionism and Emotional Symptoms in an Adolescent Sample. *Australian Journal of Psychology, 52*, 2, 89–93, August.

Gibson, L. (2004). *Avoidance*. Vermont, USA: National Center for post-traumatic stress Disorder, Department of Veterans Affairs. Fact Sheet. 2004.

Guar, C. B., Murthy, A. & Nathawat, S. S. (2001). Intelligence and scholastic achievement as determinants of stress and adjustment in adolescent male female students. *Indian J Clin Psychol, 28*, 257–263.

Hall, G. S. (1904). Adolescence: its psychology and its relations to physiology, anthropology, sociology, sex, crime, religion and education. *Classics in the History of Psychology, 2.*

Hardy, L. (2003). Overburdened, overwhelmed. *American School Board Journal, 190* (4), 18–23.

Hayes, S. C., Wilson, K. G., Gifford, E. V., Follette, V. M. & Strosahl, K. D. (1996). Emotional avoidance and behavioural disorders: A functional dimensional approach to diagnosis and treatment. *Journal of Clinical Psychology, 64*, 1152–1168.

Higgins, E. T. (1987). Self-discrepancy: A theory relating self and affect. *Psychological Review, 94*, 319–340.

Kai-Wen, C. (2009). A study of stress among college students in Taiwan. *Journal of Academic and Business Ethics, 2*, 1–8.

Lalwani, S., Sharma, G. A., Kabra, S. K., Girdhar, S. & Dogra, T. D. (2004). Suicide among children and adolescents in south Delhi (1991–2000). *Indian J Pediatr, 71*, 701–703.

Latha, K. S. & Reddy, H. (2006). Patterns of stress, coping styles and social support among adolescents. *Journal of Indian Assoc Child Adolesc Ment Health*, 3, 5–10.

Little Flower, A., Vazir, S., Fernandez Rao, S., Rao, V., Laxmaiah, A. & Nair, K. M. (2011). Percieved stress, life events & coping among higher secondary students of Hyderabad, India: a pilot study. *Indian Journal of Medical Research*, 134, July, 61–68.

Logaraj, M., Felix, J. W. & Vedapriya, D. R. (2005). Attempted suicide in adolescents reported at a medical college hospital in Tamil Nadu—some observations. *Indian Journal of Prev Soc Med*, 36, 68–72.

Muuss, R. E. (2006). *Theories of Adolescence* (6th edn). New York: McGraw-Hill Publishers.

Pitzer, R. L. (1985). Supporting Distressed Young People (publication HE-FS-2786). St. Paul, MN: University of Minnesota Extension Service April 2005 | Volume 62 | Number 7.

Pope, D. C. (2001). "Doing school": how we are creating a generation of stressed out, materialistic, and miseducated students. New Haven: Yale University Press.

Pope, D. C. & Simon, R, (2005). Help for stressed students. *The Adolescent Learner*, April, 62, 7, 33–37.

Ramya, N. & Parthasarathy, R. (2009). A study on coping patterns of junior college students. *Indian Journal of Psychological Medicine*, 31, 45–47.

Slaby, A. & Garfinkel, L. F. (1994). *No one saw my pain: why teens kill themselves*. W.W. Norton & Company.

Spira, J. C., Zvlensky, M. J., Eifert, G. H. & Feldner, M. T. (2004). Avoidance-oriented coping as a predictor of panic-related distress: a test using biological challenge. *Journal of Anxiety Disorders*, 18, 309–323.

Srikata, B. & Kumar, K. V. (2010). Empowering adolescents with life skills in schools – School mental health program: does it work? *Indian Journal of Psychiatry*, 53, 4, 344–349.

Torsheim, T. & Wold, B. (2001). School-related stress, school support, and somatic complaints: a general population study. *Journal of Adolescent Research*, 16, 3, May, 293–303.

Walker, J. (2002). *Teens in Distress Series*: Adolescent Stress and Depression. The Center for 4-H Youth Development. University of Minnesota Extension Service.

Yin, R. (1994). *Case Study Research: Design and Methods* (2nd edn). Thousand Oaks, CA: Sage Publishing.

4
Male Adolescents' Conceptions of Success, and Their Perceptions of Their School Experiences—A Case Study

Abstract: *This case study research examined the perceptions of success and the school experiences of Form Three boys in a "prestige" school (School P) in an attempt to find out why, according to their teachers, they lacked motivation. Participants were 32 students representative of the target population of 105 Form Three students. The findings indicated that while students do value many of the behaviors and attitudes associated with personal and academic success, their experiences of school left some disappointed with either quality of teaching, teacher behavior and attitudes, or the school's physical facilities. They all identified morals and values and social skills promoted by the school. Academic success was their main goal but there was a gap between that goal and teachers' perceptions of student motivation to succeed.*

Yamin-Ali, Jennifer. *Data-Driven Decision-Making in Schools: Lessons from Trinidad.* New York: Palgrave Macmillan, 2014. DOI: 10.1057/9781137412393.0008.

Introduction and background

Adolescent male low academic performance has been the source of much concern internationally and more so in the lower socio-economic strata. However, low motivation in young male adolescents has also been a challenge to teachers in the school system globally. There are many factors that may contribute to low motivation among young male adolescents which may be physiological, psychological, or sociological in nature. Eccles and Midgley (1989) believe that it is only by understanding how these three areas are interrelated that we can better understand the special and unique nature of early adolescence.

In the early secondary school years students are in the phase of adolescent maturation where they establish their own beliefs, values, and life goals. Their constant self-appraisal of themselves is often characterized as being extremely self-conscious. Piagetian psychological theory proposes that during early adolescence (ages 11–13), a new self-image is developed due to their physiological changes. Adolescents normally begin to make use of their newly acquired skills of logical thinking and ability to make rational judgments. At mid-adolescence (ages 14–15), adolescents seek to function independently of their parents, and their emotions and intellectual capacities increase. They are prone to being adventuresome in activity and in thought. It is in this period that there is struggle with their own set of values versus the set established by figures of authority such as parents and teachers, and they begin to make their own decisions about educational and vocational pursuits. However, as "independent" as adolescents may appear to be, socio-structural factors do influence behavior, according to social cognitive theory (Bandura, 1986; 1999).

According to Pintrich (2003) the term "motivation" is derived from the Latin verb *movere*, which means to move. He suggests that motivational theories attempt to answer questions about what gets individuals moving (energization) and toward what activities or tasks or direction (Pintrich & Schunk, 2002). Pintrich adds that Higgins and Kruglanski (2000) suggest that this is summed up in the central question of what individuals want and whether there are basic needs that define what people want.

Adolescent development and its attendant challenges in the academic sphere have received the attention of many researchers over recent decades (Higgins & Parsons, 1983; Simmons & Blyth, 1987; Eccles & Midgley, 1989; Ames, 1992; Pajares & Urdan, 2002). There has been much discussion about the declining academic performance of adolescents in schools, and views have been proffered as to whether pubertal development and the accompanying onset of operational thought, or the significant biological and psychological changes are major determinants of the upheaval characteristic of many adolescents in school. Cognitive social theory, and more specifically, stage-environment fit theory suggest that the environment, inclusive of family and broader social structures, also shapes the way adolescents perceive the world and respond to situations. Gutman and Eccles (2007) suggest that when considering the stage-environment fit theory, researchers should examine both the definition of "fit" in light of the characteristics of the adolescents themselves, and the amount and level of change in their family environments.

The decline in early adolescent academic performance has been noted since 1987 by Simmons and Blyth (1987), and by Eccles and Midgley (1989), who also found a decline in academic motivation and self-perception. The latter two issues are critical to the purpose of this study since these were the concerns raised by the teachers in the school context of this research. According to Hardré and Sullivan (2009:1) studies have shown that "motivational features are malleable and can significantly influence the engagement, learning, achievement, and future aspirations and intentions of students." Studies by Deci and Ryan (1985), Hardré and Reeve (2003), and Pintrich and Schunk (1996) have provided evidence of this. Therein lies the importance of understanding what students think and the concomitant necessity to provide a forum for the expression of their opinions and ideas if, as educators, we say that we want to effect increase in their levels of motivation.

In the context of this research, it was important to determine how students viewed the behaviors and attitudes that may be normally associated with being "successful". Abele (2003) has shown that "agency" (meaning "competence") in young adulthood is a predictor of career success, whereas "communion" (meaning "warmth") predicts involvement with family. Although Abele's target population was senior to the students in this study, it may have some pertinence to agency and communion even at the age of high school students who are beginning to set life goals.

Setting personal goals was seen to play a key role in students' attainment of grades in school (Zimmerman, Bandura, & Martinez-Pons 1992). Earlier research by Bandura (1992) and Locke and Lathman (1990) showed that when students' perceived self-efficacy was high, the goals they set for themselves were also high. It was seen by Zimmerman et al. (1992) that parents' influence on students' grade goals was tempered by the students' beliefs in their own academic efficacy. They also concluded that a determinant of student aspirations is their belief in their own academic efficacy. They suggest that setting demanding standards for students is not enough. Instead, learning experiences need to be structured in ways that enhance students' sense of efficacy.

A major assumption of this study is that certain attitudes and behaviors play a role in determining success inclusive of academic success. In a study of elementary to middle school students, Kiefer and Ryan (2011) found that for all students the general trend in beliefs about socially acceptable behavior was that sincere behavior remained a top-rated characteristic, and dominant and disingenuous behavior remained at the bottom. This study included girls and boys, with the latter finding these behaviors to be less important to social success when compared to the girls.

Especially in the school setting, peer influence is a significant factor to be considered in any examination of student attitudes and behaviors. According to Fadell and Temkow (n.d.), peer influence and conformity play an important and substantial role in the life of an adolescent in the context of non-academic behaviors. They propose that a consideration of contagion theory helps in the understanding of the "spread" of emotions, attitudes, and behaviors among peers and also emphasizes the importance of identifying which adolescents are more prone to contagion. The contagion factor, with proper strategizing, can be used to the benefit of students in the school setting with regard to building positive attitudes and behaviors.

In light of the fact that students in this research context would have entered this secondary school with high expectations of achievement and extra-curricular involvement, it is worth noting that Eccles and Midgley (1989) introduce the notion of person-environment fit in their study of academic motivation, observing that one can expect negative motivational consequences for individuals when they are in an environment that does not fit well with their needs. They suggest the need to examine the opportunities provided for adolescents in junior high school to ensure that their needs are being met. According to Mansfield and Wosnitza (2010), there is the possibility that broad social or cultural variables may influence students' goals since they found that in two school settings in the same region in Western Australia, student responses consistently rated responsibility goals high and status goals (fitting in with peer group) low.

Lack of person-environment fit and stage-environment fit may well result in lower-than-expected attitudes and performance in adolescent students. Eccles et al. (1993) note that negative changes in the school environment may impact negatively on adolescent motivation. When compounded by the characteristics of the developmental period, adolescents' responses to school may be unexpected and even misunderstood. Willingham (2009) suggests that students may not like school because they are frustrated or bored, but cautions that the amount of thinking required of them must be just right. He argues that higher order thinking skills essentially presume prior knowledge, which if absent, can frustrate learners. He also considers memory to be the key to thought and maintains that distractions from the objectives of a lesson must be minimized in order to promote memory. In addition, he endorses the use of practice in learning. He suggests that teachers praise effort more than ability in order to increase students' confidence.

When students try hard they expect results. Akey's research (2006) conducted in three high schools in the United States indicates that together with student engagement, students' perception of their own academic competence influenced achievement in mathematics. However, the findings also suggest that perceived academic competence may be more influential than engagement in boosting achievement in both mathematics and reading. Indeed, analyses indicate that perceived competence had a strong influence on students' perceptions of themselves as competent learners. The study concludes that supportive teachers and clear and high expectations about student behavior are key to the development of both student engagement and perceived competence and that schools should begin at a very early stage to build students' confidence in their ability to do well. This is dependent on teachers whom students see as supportive and who provide high quality instruction.

The effectiveness of the caring teacher is supported by Ryan and Patrick (2001) who studied the classroom social environment and changes in adolescents' motivation and engagement during middle high school. Their study found interaction with peers to be a positive factor in students' experience, and such interaction built their confidence in relating to their teachers also. Another conclusion of their research was that student's confidence is boosted in an environment where their ideas are respected, with little likelihood of embarrassment or teasing. Emphasis on competition within the classroom with a focus on performance was seen to be a drawback for students, and it is suggested that students could benefit from learning communication skills. They advocate better understanding of the social aspects of the classroom environment so that the marriage of social constructivist principles with research on cognitive development could guide the teacher in the classroom to increase student motivation and engagement.

With the enormous responsibility placed on the teacher to facilitate learning and overall student development, teacher effectiveness becomes the backbone of classroom learning. Goldberg (2003) highlights some of the core qualities and characteristics of great teachers as: willingness to put in the necessary time, love for the age group they teach, an effective classroom management style, positive relationships with other adults, consistent excellence, in-depth content knowledge, capacity for growth, and steadiness of purpose and teaching personality. Hardré and Sullivan (2008) add a detail to this by stating that motivating students involves both being able to diagnose whether students are motivated and to intervene in order to support or remediate.

While students have certain expectations of their teachers, depending on the socio-cultural setting, they may expect certain non-academic provision for their personal growth. The school in this study is denominational but is accessed by students of all religious persuasions. The setting is a developing nation which is multi-cultural and has deep ties to religion generally. Religion or spirituality therefore plays a major role in the lives of its citizens. In a study of 1784 high school students in Australia, Heaven and Ciarrochi (2007:691) concluded that "religious teenagers are better equipped to meet life's experiences and challenges and are therefore much less likely to be preoccupied with memories or worries, and much more likely to engage significant life issues." They suggest that "the lens through which religious adolescents perceive and make meaning of the world is not only very different from that of less religious youth, but also able to provide the ability and inner strength and resources to deal successfully with life's experiences. This is a critical advantage as adolescents in the mid-high school years confront perplexing issues related to their future, their sexuality, faith and political orientation, as they approach the transition to early adulthood" (2007, 691).

Apart from expectations of exposure to religious principles, students of "prestige schools" may expect a high standard of physical facilities. According to Kumar et al. (2008), not many studies have examined the role of the school physical environment in determining student behaviors, specifically middle and high school students' problem behaviors.

Results from their study suggest that the school physical setting through its multiple dimensions, conveys different meanings and messages for students. A school with attractive and clean classrooms gives students the impression that this is a place where their learning and growth are both valued and supported. Displays of student artwork promote a feeling of belonging and appreciation. On the other hand, schools with areas that are difficult to monitor may not be able to easily discourage negative behavior. Kumar et al. (2008) also conclude that unclean classrooms and unattractive school settings can make students feel neglected and uncared for, resulting in higher levels of truancy.

The literature on student motivation, student academic performance, and adolescent development in general, while providing rich and relevant details from diverse scenarios, leaves a gap where students' views are concerned. This study opens the window to a socio-cultural context that may preclude scrutiny of a school type which is largely perceived as "successful", "prestigious," and close to "ideal". The students are among the highest performers academically in the country and the school offers a wide range of extra- and co-curricular activities. Yet, there are concerns from the inside. This study provides the "voices" of some of the teachers but mainly those of the students in the school under study, using their experiences, perceptions, and opinions to stimulate further exploration of teachers' concerns about low student motivation at the school.

This research seeks to find out what are Form Three students' perceptions of success as well as what their school experiences are in order to understand what motivates them to be successful. It can be seen to be a forerunner to further research in school settings where school leadership or teacher complacency runs the risk of stifling student capability.

Methodology

This is a descriptive single case study which employs both qualitative and quantitative methods of data collection and analysis. It typically examines a contemporary phenomenon as it exists in its own context. The phenomenon and its context are so inextricably interwoven that it is difficult to distinguish boundaries between both (Yin, 1994). This approach, according to Yin, is suitable for studying complex social phenomena. The phenomenon being studied in this case is that of student motivation, which is impacted by many variables.

The focus is on adolescent male students' perceptions and experiences as possible determinants of their level of motivation. It is situated in a social context where historically, education has played a major role in social mobility. The context is Trinidad, a post-colonial and post-Independence developing nation, where there is much competition to gain entry into what society perceives to be the best schools. Students have some opportunity to select their preferred school, but access depends on their performance on a national achievement examination.

This study of student motivation at the Form Three level came about through the concerns of three teachers who were randomly approached to discuss an area of school life which they felt needed some sort of analysis and possible intervention. They all agreed that student motivation at the Form Three level (3rd year of secondary school) was a great concern to them. Thus, with their support, this study was elaborated.

This research ultimately seeks to investigate Form Three students' school experiences and views of school and success to better understand why, according to their teachers, they seem under-motivated.

The questions guiding the study were:

1. How do students of school P define success with regard to their own lives?
2. How do students of school P describe their experiences of school?
3. What motivates students of school P to be diligent with regard to all aspects of the school curriculum?

The researcher developed a research plan with the team, elaborated all the data collection instruments and shared it with the team for their input. The team of three teachers between themselves conducted a focus group interview with Form Three students to glean some general information about the main issues. These interviews were driven by a semi-structured guide, allowing for the interviewers to converse in a natural way based on the responses and comments being presented by the students. These interviews were transcribed and together with the researcher's ideas, the main ideas were used to develop two sections of closed ended questions on the questionnaire for the target group of Form Three students (N-105). One section sought responses about the importance of certain attitudes and behaviors in determining what a "successful" person is, and the other section sought their responses about to what extent they recognized those attitudes and behaviors in themselves. The open-ended questions were designed to allow students to provide details of their experiences, feelings, and opinions about the school and school life. The questionnaire was then administered to a pilot sample of 10 random students from the entire Form Three population. The pilot allowed for review and amendments for administering to a convenience sample of 32 Form Three students representing each of the three Form Three classes. The students filled out the questionnaires anonymously. The anonymity factor was an attempt to encourage honest answers and to remove any feeling of threat that the students may have felt in light of criticisms that they may have wanted to make.

Descriptive statistics were used to analyze the closed-ended questions. Patterns and trends were sought through that analysis as well. For the open-ended questions recurring themes were recognized and categorized having used both pre-defined and emergent codes.

Findings are presented below according to the research questions.

Findings

Research Question 1: How do students of School P define success with regard to their own lives?

Attitudes and behaviors in the context of success

The largest number of students placed a high priority on attaining goals, good academic performance, extra-curricular involvement, and dealing positively with failure. Interestingly, significantly more students felt that interacting well with people, doing things that are good for them or for others even though they are not confident they can do them, being able to admit when they are wrong, being open-minded and tolerant, and being able to sense when others respect them were not "very important" but just "important".

Students who found certain attitudes and behaviors "not too important"

As determinants of whether they were successful persons, certain criteria were not deemed important by a few students. Eight out of thirty-two students felt that being able to sense that others respected them was not important and five of them felt that being able to admit when they were wrong was not important. Four did not value as important to their success doing things that are good for them or for others even though they are not confident they can do them. Even though these numbers are small, when one considers that the total number of respondents (32) can comprise one class, it is evident that trying to develop the "whole" student with a view to being successful as a person can be a challenge for a teacher.

Students' self reports of their attitudes and behaviors in the context of being a successful person

Most students reported that they demonstrated these attitudes and behaviors either all of the time or sometimes. Those that seemed difficult to maintain all of the time were *attaining the major goals they set out to achieve*—21 could do this only sometimes and one could hardly do so; *being able to admit when they were wrong*—nine did so all the time, while 21 did so sometimes and two hardly; *being well focused* was constant for 15 of the students while the same number maintained their focus only sometimes and two hardly; only 11 students were *open-minded and tolerant* all of the time while 20 were so sometimes and one hardly; eight could *sense all the time that others respected them*, but 21 could do so only sometimes, while two could hardly do so and one could not do so at all; only nine students could *manage their time well* all of the time, while 19 could do this sometimes and four could hardly achieve this; 12 of them were able to *get to the root of their failure or problems* all of the time, while 19 were able to do so sometimes and one was hardly able to do so; 11 always *seek help when necessary*, and 15 did so sometimes, while three hardly seek help.

Areas of concern

There were one or two students who *hardly* demonstrated one or more of the following attitudes and behaviors: attain the goals they set out to achieve, do whatever they have to do to the best of their ability, interact well with people, do things on time, are able to make responsible and effective decisions by thinking things out carefully, pick themselves up and move ahead when they fail, are able to admit when they are wrong, are well focused, are open-minded and tolerant, try to help others, can sense that others respect them, enjoy what they do in and out of school, perform well academically, and try to get to the root of their failure or problems. Three are humble although proud of themselves and three hardly seek help when necessary. Four of them hardly manage their time well. One never senses that others respect him, and one is not at all involved in activities other than academics. Such small pockets of students have the capacity to influence the tone of a class either by challenging the teachers' management capability or the other students' understanding and tolerance.

Reasons students gave for the gap between their beliefs and their actual attitudes and behaviors

One student who felt that interacting well with people was important hardly interacts well "because I feel too much interaction will impede my learning and prevent me from achieving my goals in life," and another who felt it was very important to interact well with people hardly did so because "people do not respect my likes, dislikes and various talents." Another student who felt that seeking help when necessary was not too important hardly does so because of "confidentiality."

Among the students who gave reasons for gaps in beliefs and actuality, Student M commented most frequently on gaps in his situation. He commented five times. He explained that although he believed that doing whatever he had to do to the best of his ability was important, he hardly did so because he was lazy. He also thought that it is very important to pick oneself up after failure and move ahead but he hardly practices this because "its [sic] too hard when other persons are not there to motivate and assist you". He saw that being well-focused was very important but he is hardly focused because "my laziness and negative mindset usually holds [sic] me back." In addition, he thought that being humble while being proud of oneself was very important, but he conveyed that he is not proud of himself "as I view all my actions good or bad in the same light." Excessive amounts of homework make school less enjoyable, as well as his parents being "protective".

Summary

Overall, most students recognized that essential attitudes and behaviors are important ingredients of being successful, and most of them said that their lives reflected these either sometimes or all the time. While it is normal that a few students did not fall into these categories, it is useful for teachers to know that these students are aware of their attitudes and behaviors and that some are able to offer explanations or reasons for them.

Research Question 2: How do students of school P describe their experiences of school?

Did the school meet their expectations?

Nineteen students said that the school did not meet their expectations. Of those 19, one comment was positive: "I thought it would have been strict but it is normal and everyone knows when to play and when to do schoolwork." Of those who said that it did not meet their expectations, 10 of them mentioned facilities as the major disappointment: "better toilet facilities"; "desks"; "chairs"; "better facilities for learning"; "the school is dilapidated"; "classes are not modern."

A disappointment turned out to be a positive experience for one student who said that "they try to get you to fail via their tests...but I like my school the way it is as I have realized that from failures you learn important lessons."

Some students were disappointed by behavior and attitudes of others: "Behavior and respect is [sic] very low"; "I am surrounded by persons who couldn't care less and who have no regard for personal property or other persons"; "some students exhibit negative demeanor"; "some students have bad personalities."

Four students made negative comments about teachers: "It is full of 'wajang',[1] delinquent teachers"; "some of the members of staff are lazy and don't teach"; "poor teaching staff"; "some teachers are not understanding at all."

Thirteen students felt that the school had met their positive expectations including four who said that it has turned out to be even better. Those four comments were "The school has created a spirit within me which allows me to enjoy school and look forward to coming to school. The atmosphere is enjoyable and fun"; "Extra Curricular activities such as football and cricket clubs"; "it gave me high expectations of what a school would be"; "it was better than I expected."

Those who felt that the school turned out as positively as they thought it would cited varied reasons: "the academic quality is good"; "a big school with beautiful scenery"; "the school is very all-rounded with its academics and sports etc. There are helpful teachers and a tranquil environment"; "it has great teachers"; "the persistence and skill of the teachers as well as the success of the students in terms of scholarships"; "I do well in my work with little effort"; "it performs well and has a high standard"; "I have understood my work better and grown as a student as I would have expected."

Summary

There were mixed feelings about students' expectations of the school. There were disappointments, higher expectations in terms of facilities and teaching, but on the other hand there were several students who were satisfied with the teaching and learning, as well as the extra-curricular activities and school setting.

What students do not like about school

What students do not like about their experience at school fell under seven broad categories:

1 Facilities—12 complaints about facilities included discomfort due to a hot auditorium, "disastrous" state of football field", hot classrooms, leaking roof in classroom, unclean washrooms, classroom furniture, insufficient labs, unavailability of recreational areas.
2 Other students—"insults by students," "students who do not have respect for your hobbies and personal possessions," "bullying, inappropriate behavior and obscenities," "verbal violence."
3 Assembly—five students disliked afternoon assembly and one other also disliked morning assembly.
4 Lack of attention to sports—"sport is not a vital thing for the school," "there should be more sporting facilities."
6 Teachers—"when teachers do not come to class to teach," "the attitudes of teachers towards the students," "I do not like unpleasant teachers," "the senseless way some teachers behave."
7 Administration—"the almost dictatorial student-administration relationship"
8 School philosophy—"the school's passion for a perfect school, something attainable to them"

Subjects that they needed to try harder at and why

It is evident that the majority of the students felt that more effort was needed in order to improve their grades. There are two types of students, though: those who are not performing well and wish to improve, and those who are performing satisfactorily or well, but wish to do even better. The students do demonstrate a level of motivation to improve or to excel academically.

Research Question 3: What motivates students of this school to be diligent with regard to all aspects of the school curriculum?

The factors that motivate students to try hard fell under eight broad categories: personal satisfaction, competition, academic, challenge, career, support, teaching factors, and holistic development.

Why students are motivated to work hard at certain subjects

Students identified specific reasons for working hard at specific subjects. These reasons included the following: "the difficulty," "my aspirations," "the subjects...have a link to my hobbies," "the desire to perform well academically," "teachers," "how it applies to my life," "how interesting they are to me," "they are my favorite subjects," "I want to be successful," "I am fuelled by a desire to learn more," "I like them," "my low academic performance," "the challenge of doing well," to have "a good future," "the teachers' attitude," "teachers' and parents' expectations," "the diligent teachers," "the encouragement I get from the teacher," "I know it can expand my limits as a person."

Even if they didn't like a subject, some students were able to offer reasons for trying hard to do well in them: "to get a good grade overall," "to try to understand it," "a good teacher, willing, able and patient," "parents," "friends' support," "competitiveness," "making it fun and enjoyable." Most of the students were interested in better overall performance to achieve their academic goals such as "increasing my percentage." One student would try hard in order to "place first in test."

Why students enjoy classes

Students seem to enjoy interactive classes (this may mean that they have the opportunity to engage in activities in addition to listening, writing, and speaking), classes where there is a feeling of fun in the classroom, with teachers whom they perceive to be effective, and with subject matter which they find new, exciting and even challenging.

The classes students work best in and why

There were students who work best at certain subjects because of their natural interest or ability in them. Others were positively influenced in their output by their teachers' performance and attitude, and interaction in class. However, it cannot be determined by this study whether the students' environment (teachers and classroom activity) was the cause of their feeling that the subject was "easy" or that they were "good at it."

Why students do not enjoy classes

In some cases, the lack of enjoyment of a subject had to do with the students' experience and perception of the teacher including teachers' attitude and behavior, and in other instances, it had to do with the way the subject was being taught including types of activities, amount of practice, and usefulness of activities. Note-taking and too much homework were specific examples given.

Non-academic areas students would like to develop more

In addition to recognizing that certain attitudes and behaviors were very important to personal success, student responses also highlight four non-academic areas which they recognize as gaps in their personal development. The following broad areas were those highlighted in descending order of frequency:

Spiritual life
Social life
Family life
Personality and physical self

Yet, when they were asked to comment on what they learn at school that helps to make them successful persons, individually they were able to identify the specific areas below:

- integrity;
- honesty;
- moral teaching (assembly);
- social skills;
- morals;
- interact with other people;
- not to be selfish/generous;
- to be respectful;
- to have an open mind;
- that a successful person is holistic;
- understanding of social acceptance/rejection;
- teachers' support of students;
- to communicate better;
- to develop my social life;
- discipline;
- important values;
- to embrace other cultures and ideas;
- life lessons (teachers give us tips);
- ethics;
- kind-heartedness of most of our teachers inspires us;
- discipline;
- respect;
- school cheer;
- support;

- being friendly;
- inspirational messages;
- attitude.

Morals and values, and social skills were mentioned most frequently. Apart from four students who did not respond to this question, there were no responses that reflected a negative experience at the school. However, there seems to be a need for more exposure to non-academic avenues to personal student success.

Discussion and conclusion

The findings of this study point to several areas of students' perspectives on their own motivation and school experiences that may drive curriculum planning and school policy at this school. Equally interesting is the fact that the focus of this research was initiated by teachers of the school, which reflects the view of Hardré and Sullivan (2008) that motivating students has to do with diagnosing their level of motivation in order to intervene meaningfully.

Bearing in mind that this study originated with teachers' concern that Form Three boys (14–15 yrs of age) seem to lack motivation in their studies, the findings indicate that in the first place, most of the students chose this school because they considered it to be the "top" or "best" school either in the country or in the region. They had been clearly motivated to work hard at the primary level to gain entry into this school since entry is competitive. It can be said that these students did begin their secondary school career with personal goals which, to a large extent include examination grades (Zimmerman et al., 1992). All of them were open about what they needed to try hardest at in school in terms of academics and expressed a desire to improve. It would seem that by and large these students believed in themselves and had high aspirations, both academically and non-academically. This supports the view of Bandura (1992) and Locke and Lathman (1990) that when perceived self-efficacy is high, the goals students set for themselves are also high. In addition, their perceived academic competence was high. This in itself could possibly boost achievement (Akey, 2006).

As predictable as it may have been, the students were also very expressive about their dissatisfactions and disappointments with regard to deficiencies in either their academic performance or personal development.

Some of the students' responses about being "bored" and preferring teachers to "keep on the topic" support Willingham's (2009) views that student frustration and boredom must be tempered by the right amount of "thinking," and that distractions in class can serve to impede memory. The student view that "there is not enough practice" is also endorsed by Willingham (2009).

The range of students' dissatisfaction and disappointments in terms of school facilities and teacher performance suggests that in some cases, there is a person-environment misfit (Eccles & Midgley, 1989). This may be so specifically with regard to the expectations students have of the provision of sporting facilities at the school. Other complaints related to school facilities remind us of the role of the physical environment in encouraging positive student thinking and behaviors (Kumar, O'Malley, & Johnston 2008). The kinds of reasons these students cited for not enjoying classes as opposed to the reasons they gave for enjoying other classes are an indication that supportive teachers can build students' engagement and self-confidence (Akey, 2006). Some students' comments also reflected a need for teachers to exhibit more professional behavior by displaying more respect for students, and by demonstrating more responsible behavior, reminiscent of the effectiveness of caring teachers and their understanding of the social realm of teaching (Ryan & Patrick, 2001). Students' comments also reinforced Goldberg's (2003) emphasis on teacher effectiveness as the backbone of learning.

This study enabled students to take an inward look at themselves with a view to determining gaps in their development, not just academically but personally and socially. Almost all the students recognized some degree of importance of attitudes and behaviors that contribute to personal success, and were also able to evaluate to what extent these are reflected in their lives. The results indicate a degree of commonality with the finding of Kiefer and Ryan (2011) that, among students of similar age, sincere behavior was highly valued as socially acceptable behavior. In terms of self-management and interaction with others, while contagion theory offers suggestions about positive influence (Fadell & Temkow, n.d.), there is the consideration that as in any other context, social and cultural variables may be a factor in determining these students' views on life and of themselves (Mansfield & Wosnitza, 2010). The data show that they generally do have high personal standards which may come from their upbringing. Most of them were able to identify non-academic positive influences in their school life, and indicated a desire to develop more spiritually, echoing the possibility that confusion and anxiety are lessened through the development of inner strength (Heaven & Ciarrochi, 2007).

The outcomes of this research highlight the reality that, as in this context, students are often misunderstood since teachers misread their output in class and in assessments. In this school setting it is likely that just as students have expectations of the school, teachers have certain expectations of students, and form judgments based on these expectations without examining the needs of individual students. That these students have all accessed entry into this "prestige" school may account for teachers' approach to them in a "carte blanche" manner. It may well be that some of the students exhibit a lack of motivation due to their disappointment with certain variables in their school experience. Whether there is a causal relationship between motivation and disappointment opens the way for further research in this setting. On a final note, when teachers identify challenges in their teaching that they wish to explore, they need to be open to unexpected findings which need to be addressed.

Note

1 Wajang—colloquial word for "hooligan-like".

References

Abele, A. E. (2003). The dynamics of masculine-agentic and feminine communal traits: findings from a prospective study. *Journal of Personality and Social Psychology, 85*, 768–776.

Akey, T. M. (2006). *School Context, Student Attitudes and Behavior, and Academic Achievement: An Exploratory Analysis*. MDRC.

Ames, C. (1992). Classrooms: goals, structures, and student motivation. *Journal of Educational Psychology, 84*, 3, 261–271.

Bandura, A. (1986). *Social Foundations of Thought and Action: A Social Cognitive Theory*. Englewood Cliffs, NJ: Prentice Hall.

Bandura, A. (1992). Exercise of personal agency through the self-efficacy mechanisms. In R. Schwarzer (Ed.), *Self-Efficacy: Thought Control of Action*. Washington, DC: Hemisphere.

Bandura, A. (1999). Social cognitive theory of personality. In L. Pervin & O. John (Eds.), *Handbook of Personality* (2nd edn, pp. 154–196). New York: Guilford Press.

Deci, E. L., & Ryan, R. M. (1985). *Intrinsic Motivation and Self-Determination in Human Behavior.* New York: Plenum.

Eccles, J. S., & Midgley, C. (1989). Stage-environment fit: developmentally for early adolescents. In R. E. Ames & C. Ames (Eds.), *Research on Motivation in Education, 3*, pp. 139–186. New York: Academic Press.

Eccles, J. S., Midgley, C., Wigfield, A., Buchanan, M., Reuman, D., Flanagan, C., & Mac Iver, D. (1993). Development during adolescence the impact of stage-environment fit on young adolescents' experiences in schools and in families. *American Psychologist*, February, *48*, 2, 90–101.

Fadell L. W. & Temkow, S. E. (n.d.). A framework for understanding peer influence among adolescents. Wayne State University. http://www.drchrustowski.com/peer_influence_paper_final.pdf, accessed May 9, 2012.

Goldberg, M. F. (2003). Keeping good teachers. In *The Qualities of Great Teachers*, ed. M. Scherer. Alexandria, VA: Association for Supervision and Curriculum Development.

Gutman, L. M. & Eccles, J. S. (2007). Stage-environment fit during adolescence: trajectories of family relations and adolescent outcomes. *Developmental Psychology, 43*, 2, 522–537.

Hardré, P. L. (2003). Beyond two decades of motivation: a review of the research and practice in instructional design and human performance technology. *Human Resource Development Review 8*, 1: 54–81.

Hardré, P. L., & Reeve, J. (2003). A motivational model of rural students' intentions to persist in, versus drop out, of high school. *Journal of Educational Psychology, 95*, 2, 347–356.

Hardré, P. L., & Sullivan, D. W. (2008). Teachers' perceptions and individual differences: how they influence teachers' motivating strategies. *Journal of Teaching and Teacher Education, 4*, 7: 1–17.

Hardré, P. L., & Sullivan, D. W. (2009). Motivating adolescents: teachers' beliefs, perceptions and classroom practices. *Teacher Development, 13*, 1, February, 1–16.

Heaven, P.C.L., & Ciarrochi, J. (2007) Personality and religious values among adolescents: a three-wave longitudinal analysis. *British Journal of Psychology, 98*, 681–694.

Higgins, E. T., & Kruglanski, A. (2000). Motivational science: the nature and functions of wanting. In E. T. Higgins & A. Kruglanski (eds), *Motivational Science: Social and Personality Perspectives* (pp. 1–20). Philadelphia: Psychology Press.

Higgins, E. T., & Parsons, J. E. (1983). Social cognition and the social life of the child: stages as subcultures'. In E. T. Higgins, D. N. Ruble, & W. W. Hartup (Eds.), *Social Cognition and Social Development* (pp. 15–62). New York: Cambridge University Press.

Kiefer, S. M. & Ryan, A. M. (2011) Students' perceptions of characteristics associated with social success: changes during early adolescence. *Journal of Applied Developmental Psychology, 32,* July–August, 218–226.

Kumar, R., O'Malley, P. M., & Johnston, P. D. (2008) Association between physical environment of secondary schools and student problem behavior. *Environment and Behavior, 40, 4,* 455–486.

Locke, E. A., & Latham, G. P. (1990). *A Theory of Goal Setting and Task Performance.* Englewood Cliffs, NJ: Prentice-Hall.

Mansfield, C. F. & Wosnitza, M. (2010). Motivation goals during adolescence: a cross- sectional perspective. *Issues in Educational Research, 20, 2.*

Pajares, F., & Urdan, T. (Eds.). (2002). *Academic Motivation of Adolescents.* Greenwich, CT: IAP.

Pintrich, P. R. (2003). A motivational science perspective on the role of student motivation in learning and teaching contexts. *Journal of Educational Psychology 2003, 95, 4,* 667–686.

Pintrich, P. R., & Schunk, D. H. (1996). *Motivation in Education: Theory, Research, and Applications.* Englewood Cliffs, NJ: Prentice-Hall.

Ryan, A. M., & Patrick, H. (2001). The classroom social environment and changes in adolescents' motivation and engagement during middle school. *American Educational Research Journal, 38,* 437–460.

Simmons, R. G., & Blyth, D. A. (1987). *Moving into Adolescence: The Impact of Pubertal Change and School Context.* Hawthorne, NJ: Aldine.

Willingham, D. (2009). *Why Don't Students Like School?* San Francisco: Josey Bass.

Zimmerman, B. J., Bandura, A. & Martinez-Pons, M. (1992). Self-motivation for academic attainment: the role of self-efficacy beliefs and personal goal setting. *American Educational Research Journal, 29, 3,* Autumn, 663–676.

Yin, R. (1994). Case Study Research: *Design and Methods* (2nd edn). Thousand Oaks, CA: Sage Publishing.

5
Subject Selection at the Secondary School Level – A Case Study

Abstract: *This case study focuses on subject selection in a secondary school (School S) in Trinidad. Feedback from 77 Form Four students and 54 Lower Six students revealed that more than half of the Form four students were not satisfied with their subject selection, and there was evidence of some mismatch between students' career preferences and their subject selection. Parents were the source of advice on subject selection for a large number of students at both levels. Lower Six students were more satisfied than those of Form Four with the choices they made. Generally, students felt they needed more options in the subject offerings. Some teachers felt that procedures for entry into Form Six need to be more just and that more transparency is needed in the subject selection process.*

Yamin-Ali, Jennifer. *Data-Driven Decision-Making in Schools: Lessons from Trinidad*. New York: Palgrave Macmillan, 2014. DOI: 10.1057/9781137412393.0009.

Introduction and background

A review of the literature in this chapter reveals that subject selection has been an issue facing students in schools in Australia, Kenya, the UK, and Canada. More than likely, this is a phenomenon that poses a challenge in many more locations.

Career choice for adolescents can be daunting in a global context that is increasingly dynamic. While adults attempt to direct their goals and aspirations, there are also covert influences that shape where young people imagine themselves as adults. When compared with developed countries, developing countries may have equally challenging situations when it comes to subject choices with a view to career planning. The setting of this research is in a rapidly developing small island, Trinidad, where the main resource has been petroleum. Thus, by and large, the population is exposed to foreign travel, media, and the cultural invasion of the United States to a large extent. There are two national universities on the island, and education is free up to the secondary level and undergraduate university level, and government assisted at the postgraduate level. Education has been a fundamental means to social mobility historically in this society.

Providing support and understanding for students who are in this phase of decision-making calls for urgent attention through school planning and policy. In a project aimed at identifying the impact of school policies and practices on students as well as other influences which affect individual subject choices and career decisions, Whiteley and Porter (1998) found that very few students had a clear idea of career or course pathways and were therefore experimenting with possibilities. The reported difficulties had to do with limited subject offerings, timetabling, and the short timeframes available to make decisions, although the impact of such constraints appeared to lessen over time.

Another study which focused on the subject choice dilemma (Tawaiyole, 2002) found that students from Papua New Guinea identified a lack of autonomy in choice of subjects at the senior secondary grades, resulting in negative feelings about not getting to study subjects they wanted to. Richardson (2008) reports positive experience, enjoyment of a subject or high examination results, and not necessarily employability or future career plans, as reasons for students opting to study English at AS-Level in the United Kingdom. In Australia too, Care and Naylor (1984) saw a strong relationship between interest in a subject and occupational interest.

Like Richardson (2008) and Care and Naylor (1984), Tripney et al. (2010) found ability and enjoyment or interest to be determinants of subject choice, but also found further studies or future careers to be a major factor. In another study Siann, Lightbody, Nicholson, Tait, & Walsh (1998) reported that the majority of students in their sample chose subjects that they liked, with a view to future careers, or subjects where there were no other more desirable options. The tendency to make these choices from a narrow viewpoint with a short-term focus was also reported.

Reporting that the lack of academic advice has been a concern in the UK, a study by Stables and Stables (1995) revealed that female students demonstrated a relative lack of confidence despite their significantly better qualifications for A-level courses than the boys. They commented on the effect this could have on A-level choices, course success, and subsequent course and career choice, and suggest that student academic guidance at the school and college level should bear this in mind. Lack of preparedness for making decisions about subject choice at the secondary school level calls for career guidance with an emphasis on goal identification as suggested by Hodkinson and Sparkes (1993) who remind us of the adolescent tendency to change their minds in terms of vocational choice.

Linked to lack of preparedness for subject selection is the notion that the common perception of certain subjects may decrease the motivation to pursue them. The example cited by Wikeley and Stables (1999) within the UK is the diminished popularity and perceived importance of modern languages, Physical Education (PE) and Technology. Their research shows this concern to have emerged 12 years after their initial findings. New trends and social dynamics have further exacerbated the conflict in guidance that students receive when deciding on subject choices and future careers.

Even when schools believe they are providing the guidance that students need to make informed subject choices, some research has shown that at least 30% of a student sample in Australia indicated that no information booklet about subject choice was given to them at school, when in fact, such a booklet had been distributed by all schools in the study (Warton & Cooney, 1997). The study also reported that subject choice information was gathered in an ad hoc manner by students. Chapman (1993) is of the view that there is need for more research on the usefulness of actual career-related resources to students. Truong, as recently as 2011, echoes Chapman's concerns when she reports on this issue in Ontario schools where although students appeared to be satisfied with the breadth of counseling coverage, they were not as satisfied with the quality of advice received. Students in the Australian context, according to Warton and Cooney (1997), are able to differentiate between information sources based on their usefulness, although their study reports that many adolescents do not seek or do not access necessary information for rational decision-making.

There may be a variety of factors that determine how students choose subjects. Ainley, Robinson, Harvey-Beavis, Elsworth, & Fleming (1994) suggest locus of control, self-assessment of ability, vocational awareness, gender, and interest in the subjects offered to be some. Informal sources of information as opposed to formal career guidance seemed to be the preferred option for students who were guided by parents and siblings (Dellar, 1994). Edwards and Quinter (2001) report similar findings in a study of students in Kenya.

In terms of how the quality of career guidance can be enhanced in schools, Truong (2011) reports that students appreciate advice, even at the end of the first year of A-Level study, about what they will do in the future, either at university or in employment. A further example of how students need help is that although the students in her study were aware that studying English at A-Level would help them to develop additional key skills, they were unsure as to how these skills are applicable.

Some of the researchers mentioned above have offered suggestions on how schools can promote better student decisions regarding subject choice. Tawaiyole (2002) suggests that the school's curriculum should be sufficiently flexible to allow students to select a broad range of subjects in order to produce graduates who are multi-skilled or qualified in more than one specialized area or discipline, thus broadening their career and life options. A focus on the employability of Humanities students is proposed by Richardson (2008) who further suggests that student visits to universities may be useful as "taster sessions".

The concept of a school-based integrated career program was developed by Gullekson (1995) over two decades ago. It provides fundamental elements of personal career development to all grade levels of the entire school population. In 2004, the then DfES (Department for Education and Skills, 2001–2007) in the UK required maintained schools in England and Wales to deliver a curriculum-based program of careers education to students in the early years of secondary school to enable them to develop career management skills earlier, to be better prepared to make decisions at a later stage. Further curriculum and qualification reforms sought to enable all young people to choose personalized pathways which suited them and which easily propelled their progression (Tripney et al., 2010). Truong in 2011 suggests a similar concept of integrating a career planning component into high school subject courses.

This study examines student response to the process of subject selection at their school as well as concerns teachers have about that process. It highlights the level of student satisfaction with their choices, their goals, how they cope with the process of subject selection, their sources of advice, and teachers' perceptions of the process. This study was proposed by some teachers from the school who were concerned about the effectiveness of the subject selection process there. The initial interest is therefore from an insider perspective.

Methodology

This research is set within a bounded descriptive case study paradigm. It is a single case featuring both qualitative and quantitative methodologies. This case study focuses on the phenomenon of subject selection in a particular school. Subject selection is not as clinical as it may seem on the surface as there are many factors that contribute to final decisions, and several players in the subject selection scenario who make the process and the experience complex at times. The case study approach allows the researcher to "portray what it is like to be in a particular situation, to catch the close-up reality and thick description of participants' lived experiences of, thoughts about and feeling for a situation" (Geertz 1973 cited in Cohen et al., 2000). The questions guiding the study were:

1 What are the outcomes of current subject choices for the Form Four level from students' perspectives?
2 What are the outcomes of current subject choices for the Form Lower Six level from students' perspectives?
3 What are the outcomes of current subject choices for the Form Four and Lower Six levels from teachers' perspectives?
4 What are students' suggestions for improved subject selection processes at the school?

The context of the study is a mixed secondary school which is church affiliated but to a large extent, is funded by the government. It was established 57 years ago and is a first choice institution in its geographical area. The broader context is Trinidad and Tobago, a developing country. In an attempt to encourage a culture of data-driven decision-making at the school, this researcher interviewed three teachers from among the school's staff in order for them to identify an issue in their school which they would like to investigate. The research process began when they agreed that their concern was decision-making with regard to subject choices for entry into Form Four and into Form Six. This concern translated into the need to find out the views of students and teachers about the effectiveness of the subject choice process. The researcher then developed a research plan with the team, designed the data collection instruments and shared them with the team for their input. Two focus group interviews with the research team and two focus group interviews, one with Form Four and one with Lower Six students informed the design of two separate questionnaires for teachers and students of Forms Four and Six. The student questionnaires were piloted before administering the final version. A telephone interview with a key member of the subject selection team was also conducted to gain a third perspective on details of the subject selection process. A semi-structured interview guide was used for this interview.

A major feature of this research was the involvement of the team of teachers in the brainstorming phase of the research. They conducted the focus interviews with students and administered the questionnaires to the larger body of students. The students' questionnaires focused on both the outcome of the selection process for students and their experience of the process as well.

Seventy-seven Form Four students and 54 Lower Six students filled out questionnaires which consisted of identical questions except for relevance to students' class level. All questionnaires were completed anonymously to encourage openness with their opinions and views.

Closed-ended questions were analyzed quantitatively while patterns and trends were also sought. Deeper insights into phenomena were achieved through comparison and cross analysis. Recurring themes and categories were generated from the qualitative data. As far as possible, synthesis of categories was realized without losing the voices of the respondents. Further analysis was made possible through comparison of responses within groups resulting, in some instances, in special focus on individual students.

Findings are presented below guided by the research questions.

Findings

Students' perspectives

Student satisfaction with subject choice

Students can enter Form Four to study eight, or in a few cases, nine subjects. English A (Language) and Math are compulsory.

Of the 77 Form Four students who responded, 31 (40%) did not get to do one or more subjects that they would have liked to do. Eleven (14%) of them would have preferred to do a certain subject for career reasons, and 20 (26%) for interest in or love for the subject. The number of times a subject was cited as "would have liked to do it but didn't get to choose it" is indicated in Table 5.1. Forty-seven (61%) students had to make "forced choices" based on the options provided. There was a total of 10 subjects which some students would have preferred not to select.

Table 5.2 indicates the number of students who chose specific subjects which they would have preferred not to study.

The types of reasons students gave for not preferring to do certain subjects are outlined in Table 5.3.

TABLE 5.1 *Number of students (out of 77) who did not get to do preferred subjects*

PE	IT	POA	Physics	Geog	Hist	Art	French	Span	Chem	POB
9	5	5	4	4	5	5	1	1	1	1

Note: PE—Physical Education; POA—Principles of Accounts; IT—Information Technology; POB—Principles of Business

TABLE 5.2 *Number of students (out of 77) who had to study subjects they would have preferred not to study*

Geog	History	Eng. Lit.	Biology	POA	Add Math	Spanish	Econ	POB	Social St.
15	9	8	8	6	6	4	3	2	1

TABLE 5.3 *Reasons students gave for not liking subjects*

Geog.	Don't like (3); don't like map reading; too much to remember; don't need it for career (4); difficult (3); confusing; boring (2)
Hist	Boring; a lot of reading; irrelevant (1); not interested; not useful; don't need it for my field; too much to remember;
Eng. Lit.	Shakespeare difficult to understand (2); don't need it for career (2); don't need to learn about stories; boring and lame; Eng A is enough-prefer another subject in its place;
Bio	Difficult (3); don't like (2); not good at it; uninteresting; not needed for my career; not inclined to Sciences; too much to remember;
POA	Too much Math; difficult to remember concepts; challenging; boring; too many rules; not good at it; don't plan to own a business
Add Math	Not my favorite subject; don't need it; preferred to do a Business subject; don't have capability; boring; difficult (2);
Spanish	Difficult to grasp (4); boring (2);
Econ	Too hard to remember; boring; a lot of drawing; no need for it;
POB	Boring; poor performance; teacher not focused
Social Studies	Irrelevant

Coping with choosing subjects

Students were asked to indicate whether they had difficulty with selecting subjects and to explain why. Of the 77 respondents, 46 (60%) students said that they had no difficulty with subject selection, 14 (18%) said that they did have difficulty, and 16 (21%) said that it was "somewhat" difficult to choose subjects. One student did not respond.

Students' difficulties with the subject selection process

Forty-six students had no difficulty with selecting subjects. Sixteen were sure of subjects they wanted, nine had a goal, three felt that "the subject choice sheet was easy to read and understand," two liked the subject, and the other reasons were that the student either "didn't have a choice," "it was simple," "the class I wanted to go to had the subjects I wanted," "parents helped," "only had 1 choice," and "everything I wanted to do was right on the paper."

Thirty students had some degree of difficulty selecting. Eight couldn't choose what they wanted and combinations prevented four from choosing. Two felt that the time to choose was short and two were unsure of their career path. There were single instances of a student who did not know "what the subject would be like," who "didn't know what subjects I needed for my field," who felt that [the sheet] "did not have all the choices," who felt "pressure from parents" or "couldn't change my mind," "wasn't sure whether I would do good in Science," "had chosen in advance but was difficult to choose backups," "had to choose with future subjects in mind," and "too many subjects with great options."

Students' goals and subject choices

Of the 61 students (79%) who indicated that they had a career in mind by the time they were at the end of Form Three, 54 (70%) chose subjects suited to their chosen career.

Sixteen students did not have a career in mind when they chose their subjects at the end of Form Three. One said, "I don't know what I would do with the subjects I'm doing now." Six of them did not seem to have chosen subjects that were suitable for their career choice. The 16 students who were not sure of their career path fell almost equally into the three groupings: Modern Studies (5), Business (5), and Science (6). There was a mismatch between the career preferences of the six students and their subject choices.

It would also seem that a total of 21 out of 77 students would drift into a career depending on their examination results after Form Five since 16 were unsure of their career direction and six would not be equipped to follow their desired career path. They would more than likely choose a career dependent on the subjects that they would be successful in. Seventy-one percent of the student sample may have already determined their career path by taking the initial step of ensuring that they had the opportunity to succeed in the subjects in their chosen field. Those 54 students are distributed among Business Studies, Modern Studies, and Science.

Advice about choosing subjects

It is evident that parents have influence over a large number of students in terms of subject choice. This indicates that career education organized by the school must include parents. What also emerges is that a significant number of students make their selections without input from an informed advisor since 19 of them said they got advice from no one. Of the 16 students who had said that they didn't know what they wanted to do after Form Five, five of them had received no advice from anyone with regard to selecting subjects. Of the 54 who were able to match their goals with their subject choices, 14 got no advice from anyone. Those 14 seem to be focused and confident about how to achieve their objectives.

In terms of parental advice, 24 of the 54 students who were able to match their goals with their subject choices indicated that they had received advice from a parent, and of that 24, eight had been advised by a parent together with someone else.

Cases that indicate a need for guidance

The following cases indicate instances where students seem to feel confused or disappointed with their current status in terms of subject choices. Sometimes it is apparent that they are unaware of requirements for career paths, or entry into Form Six or tertiary institutions. They may have benefited from more informed guidance.

Case 1—"I chose the subjects I liked and would be interested to do but I didn't get in." This student did not have a career in mind and at the end of the first semester in Form Four said "I don't know what I would do with these subjects I'm doing now."

Case 2—wanted to be a P.E. teacher but was not offered P.E. "I could pursue Nursing instead."

Case 3—wanted to pursue Civil Engineering. "I want to study Technical Drawing and Geography" after Form Five. However, this student is not pursuing these subjects in Form Four.

Case 4—initially wanted to pursue Medicine or Law. No Science subjects are in this student's profile. S/he is not studying History either and says "it would have helped in my choice of career in law." This student doesn't "know at this point" what he or she will study or do after Form Five.

Case 5—wants to study Pure/Applied Math after Form Five but is currently in the Modern Studies grouping. She says "probably to me it was unfair because you just can't put a student in business class, get them all happy/excited then just take them out and put them in Modern Studies."

Case 6—wants to study later at a School of Accounting and Management or work as an entrepreneur but is currently not studying Accounts (POA).

Case 7—had no career in mind when subjects were selected for entry into Form Four and currently does not know what he wants to study or to do after Form Five.

Case 8—wanted to become a pilot but is currently studying Business subjects with no Sciences.

Case 9—wanted to become a POA or IT teacher but is studying neither at the Form Four level. He or she still wants to pursue that exact career.

Case 10—had no career in mind at the end of Form Three and having chosen subjects in Modern Studies, does not know what to pursue or do after Form Five.

Case 11—"My dream is always and always had been to become a psychologist." His or her plan after Form Five is to "go to the school of Accounting and Management."

Case 12—career path at the end of Form Three was mechanical engineering but after Form Five plans to study History and Social Studies. S/he is currently in the Modern Studies grouping.

Case 13—"I wanted to be a doctor." Is currently in the Modern Studies grouping and now wants to work as a police officer after Form Five.

Case 14—wanted in Form Three to become a secondary school teacher of Linguistics and Social Studies. Wants to get a "Bachelor's degree in Social Studies and Geography."

Case 15—Wanted to be a gynaecologist. Is pursuing Sciences. After Form Five wants to "work as a teacher."

Form Six

Student satisfaction with subject choice

Students at the Form Six level normally have the chance to select three subjects other than compulsory ones. In special circumstances, four subjects may be allowed.

Of the 50 Form Six students who responded, very few students did not get to do a subject they would have preferred to do as indicated in Table 5.4. The number of times a subject was cited as "would have liked to do it but didn't get to choose it" is indicated in Table 5.4.

Details provided by the students did not indicate that these choices would have been the reason for not having access to their initial choice of career. They seemed to want these subjects because they liked them or

TABLE 5.4 *Number of students (out of 50) who did not get to do preferred subjects*

Math	Pure Math	IT	Soc	Eng. Lit.	Geog	Econ	Computer Science
2	2	2	1	1	1	1	1

TABLE 5.5 *Number of students (out of 50) who had to study subjects they preferred not to*

Econ	Accounts	Chemistry	Env. Science	Sociology	Math	Spanish	History	Pure Math	Bio
14 (28%)	4	2	3	2	1	2	1	1	1

they had been performing well in them. There was one case of a student who wanted to study medicine but the subjects he or she was studying were Applied Math, Physics, and Environmental Science. Ironically this student would have preferred to do Pure Math but was denied the subject. Pure Math might not have been an asset to gain entry into the field of Medicine.

On the other hand, Table 5.5 indicates the number of students who chose specific subjects which they would have preferred not to study.

It is apparent that a significantly large number of students indicate that they would prefer not to have selected Economics. Further details about why students preferred not to do certain subjects are presented below.

Subjects and students' comments

Economics: It is difficult (9); don't have a foundation; too fast paced for me; my career has nothing to do with it; a lot of work; confusing sometimes;
Accounts: It is difficult (3); not my strongest area; not very interested in it;
Chemistry: not required for any field I would enter; would rather do Physics;
Environmental Science: The SBAs[1] are tedious; not very interesting; similar to Geog—both of which I have no interest in;
Sociology: not enjoying it as I used to; plenty reading;
Math: time-consuming and tedious practice;
Spanish: I like it but it is extremely difficult; problems with sentence construction and remembering vocab;
History: very lengthy;
Pure Math: too many past papers;
Biology: too much reading.

Economics is a subject taught at the Form Six level only. Many concepts are therefore new to students at this level. It seems that many students did not know what to expect from the subject when they chose it. Bearing in mind that this feedback from students was solicited early in their entry into Lower six, their responses to the subjects at the Form Six level would have been as novices. It may indicate a need for more "weaning" into the Form Six program in terms of teaching strategy, academic advising, and general student guidance.

Coping with choosing subjects

Students were asked to indicate whether they had difficulty with selecting subjects and to explain why. Of the 50 students who responded, 36 (72%) students said that they had no difficulty with subject selection, six (12%) said that they did have difficulty, and eight (16%) said that it was "somewhat" difficult to choose subjects. Generally students who had no difficulty felt that the choices were straightforward and aligned to their choice of career. Of those who had difficulty, two weren't sure whether they corresponded to choice of career, three hadn't chosen a career, for four there were clashes for their choices, one wanted to do a subject which did not relate to his/her grouping (e.g., Biology did not go with Business), and another was torn between two career options.

Although a significantly larger number of students had no difficulty with the subject selection for entry into Form Six, the 14 students who had some sort of difficulty may have made "forced choices", thereby opening them to self-doubt, lack of confidence and perhaps lack of purpose in the particular class. This has implications for teaching strategy and teacher-student relationships as well.

Students' goals and subject choices

Generally, by the time students have qualified to enter Form Six, they have a fair idea of their career goals, or at least, an idea of whether they intend to continue their studies at the tertiary level. This is reflected in this group of Lower Six students. Of those students who indicated their choice of career, the majority had selected subjects appropriate to their chosen career. There was only one student who seemed to have a definite mismatch between his or her choice of career and the subjects selected for study at this level. This student wanted to major in Management at the university level but was studying Spanish, Sociology, and Literature at the Form Six level.

There were seven students who did not have a career in mind when they chose their subjects to enter into Form Six. Of those seven, three of them also had no idea of what they planned to do after Form Six.

When the students responded to the questionnaire they had just completed the first of six semesters in Form Six. Eight students in all had no idea of what they wanted to do after Form Six. Of those eight, three had no career in mind when they entered Form Six.

It may well be that with the challenge of gaining entry into Form Six, some students did not reach the point of making decisions about where they would be in 16 months' time. In addition, it may also simply mean that there were options from which they still had time to make a choice.

Advice about choosing subjects

It is evident that as in the case of Form Three students, a large number of parents of Form Five students have influence over their children's subject choice. Career education organized by the school for Form Five students must include parents. That seven students got advice from no one is perhaps an indication of their own focus and determination as in the case of the younger students mentioned earlier in the discussion of Form Four students.

Teachers' perspectives

Subject selection management

A key player in the subject selection process is a teacher who has been at the school for 14 years and has been involved in the management of student subject choices for that period of time. Feedback from this subject selection team member indicates that changes to the options are made periodically depending on students' needs and trends. Form Four option groupings are dependent on Form Six option groupings in that there has to be a natural flow that would enable students to move fairly easily into an appropriate cluster in Form Six. At the end of Form Three, students' marks over three terms in Form Three are considered. A career guidance day is organized where personnel from various fields are invited so that students have access to more information about certain career paths. At the end of Form Five a survey is done to ascertain students' Sixth Form subject preferences. One change in the selection sheet for Form Six has been that clusters of four subjects have been included so that students can choose three out of the four subjects in the cluster to enable more flexibility of choices. Instead of the regular three subjects, students also have the option to study four, but they are advised not to choose three subjects with labs because of the demands on their time. It is usually the Science student who would do four subjects because it opens up the opportunity to win a national scholarship. New subjects such as Environmental Sciences and Technical Drawing have been added to the choices in recent times. To support these additions, teaching time per subject has been decreased. It has been reported that teachers have had to manage their time better to cope with this decrease in teaching time. Feedback from this source states that teachers who have not been involved in the selection decision process have all supported the recent changes made on the choice sheets.

Staff on the ground

Discussions with one small cluster of teachers revealed a contradictory state of affairs with regard to the process of subject selection. There was a concern that after their final examinations at the end of Form Five, some students "just come in and choose subjects based on the grades they got" as opposed to what they really want to do, and others "would know exactly what they want to do but may not be given the subjects." That also felt that sometimes students are not aware of why they were not selected for their choices. The example cited was that there are many applications for Management of Business (MoB) and the class size has to be controlled so that there has to be a cut-off point, but students are not aware of this practicality. Another concern was about the informal phase of the process when students arrive at the school to collect their final examination results at the end of Form Five and are sent away without being given an application form because of a behavioral issue on their record. The denial of entry is not formal but unspoken.

From the perspective of this group of teachers, the system of selection should involve a wider cross section of teachers. They report that teachers in general are not privy to all the applications. It is only the "selection team" that does the pre-selection and passes the selected list to the teachers concerned. One area of discontent is that at times there are students who are not on the pre-selected list but who appear in the class.

The teachers also expressed their discontent about the process of decision-making about curriculum. The area cited was Technical Drawing, which was recently introduced. The general staff was just "informed" about it rather than consulted. They "weren't given a chance to comment. Teachers just had to accommodate the decision." "Teachers were shaken up." "Are decisions data-driven?" one asked.

It is evident that although one team member had the impression that there was full staff support for subject choice decisions, there were, in fact, undercurrents of disillusion with the process of decision-making.

Student suggestions

Suggestions from Form Four students

Of the 77 students who responded to the questionnaire, 17 made no suggestion concerning the way subjects are chosen at the end of Form Three. This is apart from the seven who were satisfied with the overall process. Other than that, the suggestion that there should be freer choice occurred 13 times, with comments such as "we should be allowed to choose all of the subjects that we want to do as a mixture, e.g. we could do Science subjects and Business subjects together." Generally, these students felt that all students should be allowed to choose whatever they wanted to do. There were 11 instances where students expressed the suggestion that either a wider range of subjects or more options be offered: "the subjects where we can choose should have more options"; "we should be able to mix subjects and more should be offered." On ten occasions, students made suggestions about either what subjects should be offered or that they should be allowed to do more subjects. Three would have liked the opportunity to do P.E., one would have liked to do French, and one Physics, and another would have liked to do another unnamed subject. One student suggested being allowed to do one or two additional subjects. One student suggested replacing some subjects with others, and perhaps related to this, two students suggested that clashes should be avoided. Three students suggested that there be fewer compulsory subjects, one each suggested that Spanish, Add Math, English Literature, and Biology should not be compulsory. It should be noted that these are compulsory within certain options. Two suggested that no subject should be compulsory. There were six comments that the selection system was unfair, and three comments indicated that it was not organized: "it is also making students wonder about themselves because a student who was placed in 4B was moved to 4M and some students from 4M moved to 4B." Two students felt that fewer subjects should be studied at this level and one felt that it should be borne in mind that some students work harder after Form Three (suggesting that their track record of performance should not be the main criterion for selection). Another felt that subjects should be chosen from Form One "so less time would be wasted," and another suggested that the Principal empathize with the students. Three students made the suggestion that teachers talk to students (and in one case, parents) before the selection process: "he can give us an idea on what would be a good choice before we choose." Although the subject selection teacher team leader indicated that there is a Career Day for the students, six students suggested a Career Day, giving the impression that it was a gap to be filled. Eight students indicated that they were satisfied with the selection process so they had no suggestions to make. Of those eight, five were Business students and three were from the Science class.

Suggestions from Form Six students

Forty-six of the fifty student respondents made at least one suggestion to the principal about the way subjects are chosen at the end of Form Five. The largest number of suggestions had to do with students' preference for more subject choices or the freedom to choose what they wanted as opposed to being constrained by subject groupings. One student thought that more freedom could be facilitated by allowing "students [to] choose subjects before the time-table is created" thereby increasing flexibility of choice. Other examples of suggestions in this category were "Let students decide what subjects they would like to do and also have more options"; "Ensure that students get what they want to do." Student "interest" as opposed to student "performance" was the underlying point in the comment "ensure that they do not discourage persons from choosing the subject that they originally wanted to choose because of their grades. They at least deserve to try!" On the other hand, five students felt that selection should be made based on grades from the CSEC (Caribbean Secondary Education Certificate) examination, while one emphasized the importance of subject teacher input by saying "get advice from the teachers for each subject." A relatively large number of comments suggested more advice being provided for students when they were selecting subjects for Form Six. Among the thirteen suggestions were "subject teachers should suggest to each individual their strongest subject so they can accomplish more instead of them choosing subjects they like instead of what they are doing good in"; "give the students a better idea of what their jobs of choice entail." Career day was also a suggestion among the category of "advice".

With regard to compulsory subjects, one student felt that they should be able to choose between Caribbean Studies and Communication Studies, and another suggested that they have a choice as to when they do these subjects (meaning in the Lower Sixth year or in the Upper Sixth year).

One student suggested to the Principal to "pay attention when parents are talking to him." This comment is assumedly made in the context of selecting subjects.

Two students felt that the selection procedure was adequate and made no suggestions, apart from the four who had no response.

Discussion and conclusion

Findings indicate a fair to large degree of student dissatisfaction with subject choices, more at the Form Four entry level than at the Form Six entry level. Whereas many of the reasons for dissatisfaction at the Form Four level revolved around forced choices, difficulty level, and lack of interest, at the Form Six level, the main reason was that students preferred not to do the subject, which happened to be the same subject in all the cases. This is in keeping with the findings of Whiteley and Porter (1998) which cited difficulties related to limited subject offerings, and rushed decision-making. It also, to some extent, concurs with Tawaiyole (2002), whose findings identified a lack of autonomy in choice of subjects at the senior secondary grades to be the cause of students' negative feelings about being denied the subjects they preferred.

At both levels, up to 21% students did experience some level of difficulty selecting subjects for reasons such as constraints due to subject groupings and uncertainty of career, the latter again reflecting the findings of Whiteley and Porter (1998). Nevertheless, there were cases where students wanted to select subjects they liked (Richardson, 2008), but also subjects they liked which would at the same time lead to their career goals (Care & Naylor, 1984; Tripney et al., 2010). Forced choices were also reported by students as in the findings of Siann et al. (1998).

The findings of this research indicate that guidance with a view to informed subject selection, although provided by the school to some extent, is seen to be insufficient. As is suggested by Stables and Stables (1995), academic guidance should provide for students' lack of confidence in selecting what they are good at. Furthermore, the school's administration could be guided by the suggestion by Hodkinson and Sparkes (1993) that goal identification be emphasized when advising, especially as adolescents tend to vacillate between their options.

As in the studies by Dellar (1994) and Edwards and Quinter (2001), advice given to the students in this research context appears to be ad hoc to some extent, as for the students in the study by Warton and Cooney (1997). While the school did report making an effort, perhaps it is in the quality of the advice that the provision in lacking (Truong, 2011).

A now approach to subject selection may well be worth considering. Accessing resources of knowledge and experience from other schools may be a place to start, thereby bringing to life the community of learning which is yet dormant in this particular cluster setting of five schools to which this particular school belongs. Even worth considering may be the concept of a school based integrated career program (Gullekson, 1995) eventually attempted by the UK government (2001–2007), and which has again been advocated by Truong (2011).

Whatever the intervention, it is the hopes, dreams and possibilities of our young people that are of priority, and our systems need to function so as to realize these.

Note

1 SBA—School-based assessment.

References

Ainley, J., Robinson, L., Harvey-Beavis, A., Elsworth, G., & Fleming, M. (1994). "Subject choice in Years 11 and 12". Australian Government Publishing Service, Canberra.

Care, E. & Naylor, F. (1984). The factor structure of expressed preferences for school subjects. *Australian Journal of Education, 28*, 2, 145–153.

Chapman, R. (1993). Occupation information at a critical time of decision making. *Australian Journal of Career Development, 2*, 2, 31–35.

Cohen, L., Manion, L., & Morrison, K. (2000). *Research Methods in Education*. London: Routledge.

Dellar, G. (1994). The school subject selection process: a case study. *Journal of Career Development, 2*, 3, 185–204.

Edwards, K. & Quinter, M. (2001). Factors influencing students career choices among secondary school students in Kisumu municipality, Kenya. *Journal of Emerging Trends in Educational Research and Policy Studies, 2*, 2, 81–87.

Gullekson, D. (1995). Effective career education for secondary schools. *Guidance and Counselling*, 10, 2, 34–41.

Hodkinson, P. & Sparkes, A. C. (1993). Young people's career choices and careers guidance action planning: a case-study of training credits in action. *British Journal of Guidance and Counselling*, 21, 3, 246–261.

Richardson, A. (2008). "Links between post-16 subject choice and future career plans in AS-Level English students". Centre for Employability through the Humanities. University of Central Lancashire.

Siann, G., Lightbody, P., Nicholson, S., Tait, L. & Walsh, D. (1998). Talking about subject choice at secondary school and career aspirations: conversations with students of Chinese background. *British Journal of Guidance and Counselling*, 26, 2, 195–207.

Stables, A. & Stables, S. (1995). Gender differences in students' approaches to A-level subject choices and perceptions of A-level subjects: a study of first-year A-level students in a tertiary college. *Educational Research*, 37, 1.

Tawaiyole, S. P. K. (2002). "Subject choice dilemma: student perceptions about senior secondary education in Papua New Guinea". Paper presented to the International Education Research Conference, University of Queensland, Australia, 1–5 December.

Tripney, J., Newman, M., Bangpan, M., Niza, C., MacKintosh, M., & Sinclair, J. (2010). "Subject choice in STEM: Factors influencing young people (aged 14–19) in education: a systematic review of the UK literature". Evidence for Policy and Practice. Information and Co-ordinating Centre, Social Science Research Unit, Institute of Education, University of London.

Truong, H. Q. T. (2011). High school career education: policy and practice. *Canadian Journal of Educational Administration and Policy*, Issue #123.

Warton, P. M. & Cooney, G. H. (1997). Information and choice of subjects in the senior school. *British Journal of Guidance and Counselling*, 25, 3, 389–397.

Whiteley, S. & Porter, J. (1998). "Student perceptions of subject selection: Longitudinal perspectives from Queensland schools". Tertiary Entrance Procedures Authority (TEPA).

Wikeley, F. & Stables, A. (1999). Changes in school students' approaches to subject option choices: a study of pupils in the West of England in 1984 and 1996. *Educational Research*, 41, 3, 287–299.

6
Should We Re-Masculinize the Boys School? A Case Study

Abstract: *This study suggests that male students of School Q do not necessarily believe that teachers' gender is the determining factor in effective teaching and nurturing. They valued discipline and tolerance, time management, getting along with others, and handling conflict as important for their holistic development. They felt that the school developed most of these qualities and skills to a satisfactory level, and a significant number associated discipline, time management, honesty, courage, and handling conflict with their male teachers. The findings have implications for how male teachers relate to their male students and for how educators view holistic development of all students, regardless of gender.*

Yamin-Ali, Jennifer. *Data-Driven Decision-Making in Schools: Lessons from Trinidad.* New York: Palgrave Macmillan, 2014. DOI: 10.1057/9781137412393.0010.

Introduction and background

The context of this research is but one example among many internationally that reflect a dilemma regarding the relevance of teachers' gender in the context of educational provision.

Though limited to a specific small setting, the initial research issue and consequent findings are undoubtedly mirrored beyond the confines of Trinidad. This is evident in the literature examined in this chapter.

The issue of how to deal with male students has been a burning one for a long time. This is so for students at all levels especially because their levels of achievement have been so much lower than girls' in many settings. At the same time, academic achievement is but one goal of schooling. The examination of what we do in schools to adequately cater for all students highlights the need for a re-evaluation of the way we view gender. There has been much research in the past two decades that has focused on the issue of educating young males. There seem to be two major stances—one that says that we should focus on ensuring that we provide for male interests and strengths, while building the underplayed needs of young males, while the other, while not opposing this view, forcefully cautions against the essentializing of the male identity and the domination of the male hegemonic identity in the portrayal of the male. Apart from academic publications emanating out of the US, the governments of Australia and the UK have demonstrated due concern for the educational provision for male students and have facilitated research in this area through their own agencies and divisions such as their departments of Education and local universities.

The issue of the suitability of female teachers as teachers of male students is one that falls within this framework of provision for male students. Central to the discussion is whether these students need male role models (Kindler & Thompson, 1999; Smedley, 1998). A range of other controversial matters provide further reason for rational argument and further research to ascertain, for example, whether "men and boys are lost souls who are on the verge of becoming depressed, suicidal and violent offenders" (Pollack, 1999: xxi), or whether boys put on a proverbial male armor to survive in school (Biddulph, 1995), or whether male teachers are the ones who represent discipline as opposed to females. Calls for scholarly evidence to inform recruitment and for teachers' own voices to inform policy-making have been made by Burn (2001), and Martino and Frank (2006) suggest further research into the nature of masculinity and how one's interpretations can determine the pedagogical practices in schools. If we are to consider education as provision for the holistic development of students, then we would need to consider, apart from academic provision, what schools should cater for. Although this paper looks at the needs of male students at the secondary level, it cannot be ignored that there are core areas which are relevant to any student despite gender. Yet there is the ongoing debate about whether, in fact, there should be any difference in the educational provision for boys as opposed to girls (Burn, 2001; Martino & Meyenn, 2001; Skelton, 2003; Mills, Martino, & Lingard 2004; Martino & Kehler, 2006).

Although much of the gender debate about educational provision has to do with student achievement, the focus of this chapter is on the areas of holistic development separate from academic achievement, and with an emphasis on personal development. Much of the discussion on advocacy of male teachers for male students centers around the "crisis of masculinity" as cited by Smith (2004) without necessarily focusing on what is expected of a male boy, adolescent, or adult as a social being. Smith adds to this by saying that "few campaigners for increased male teacher numbers have successfully identified explicit skills or attributes male teachers bring to schools and how these might benefit both male and female students" (p. 6). Martin (2002) says that school is a place where boys learn what it means to be a boy and a man. He continues by saying that school is an ideal context for the celebration of diverse kinds of men in a way that gives permission for boys to be whatever kind of man he wants to grow into. But if we were to zero in on specific qualities and skills which would benefit the male student we would understand why Rowe and Rowe (2002) comment that teacher gender has nothing to do with the emphasis needed on verbal reasoning and written communication skills as essential to students' cognitive, affective, and behavioral outcomes of schooling. Mills et al. (2004) also suggest that teacher gender has minimal impact on the quality of schooling. However, what is taught is equally important as how it is taught and how students receive it. The attempt to achieve gender balance, more specifically, to recruit more male teachers at the primary level in the teaching service in Australia, led to a research project within one city (Smith, 2004). Its findings suggest a positive link between some positive teaching attributes and teacher gender. Out of 35 teachers and 18 administrators, 100% of the teachers and 97% of the administrators felt that schools benefit from a balance of male/female teachers. Pertinent to this study are the conclusions that by observing how male and female teachers interact in a social and work context, male students could benefit from the model. Another opinion offered was that improved diversity created by more gender balance on staff could help students develop cultural tolerance and see beyond stereotypes. In addition, according to the report, many respondents were of the opinion that male teachers' capacity to develop empathy with disruptive male students justified the presence of an adequate male presence on the teaching staff. Other areas in which the survey highlighted positive skills/attributes which male teachers demonstrate were their experience and special interests (which could enhance teacher/student relationships), a positive role model where physical attributes are melded with a caring and supportive character, the ability to engage male learners through motivation and better recognition of their learning needs, and a sense of humor less likely in female teachers.

Other salient factors emerge in the field. Martino and Frank (2006) drew on research into male teachers in one single sex high school in the Australian context. The discussions are undergirded by the issue of "hegemonic masculinity" and "heterosexualized masculinity" which tend to be supported by the school and the wider community. Martino and Frank challenge the "moral panic and public anxiety about the problem of failing boys" (2006, p. 19) by analyzing the "limits imposed on male teachers' pedagogical practices as a result of feeling compelled to subscribe to normalizing regimes of hegemonic heterosexual masculinity" (2006, p. 19). They cite the example of an art teacher who emphasizes that once "you get accepted, you then have influence over your students" (2006, p. 22). He plays sport to be acceptable to his students. The issue of "acceptable masculinity" also filters into the content of his teaching as he uses "boy themes". He "masculinizes" his art, according to Martino and Frank. It is as if this teacher recreates himself to get his students' attention. Another male teacher also tailors his masculinity through sport. He coaches a basketball team. In terms of discipline, Martino and Frank also highlighted that firm discipline is seen to be the expectation of male teachers. They report that another male teacher at the same school under study claimed "that it is only after the male teacher has demonstrated that he is well-organized, fair and can control the class, that male students will take an interest in the subject" (2006, p. 25). In essence, this research by Martino and Frank serves as a cautionary warning against simplifying the gender issue in teaching boys, and advises that there is a need to investigate the impact of normative constructions of masculinity/sexuality and their effect on teaching and curriculum (2006, p. 29).

If one looks closely at the recommendations or suggestions put forward by planners, practitioners, and stakeholders in general, it would be evident that apart from classroom teaching, there are other areas that are fundamental to the academic achievement of male students. Such areas cater to the overall development of the young male. Wilson (2003), in a document commissioned by the Department for Education and Skills (DfES) in the United Kingdom, uses the National Healthy School Standard in the UK to craft an approach to raising boys' achievement in school. It is noteworthy that it is a national *healthy school* standard that is driving the objective. In the "toolkit" he provides, he includes a checklist for schools which includes specific suggestions for providing for male students' needs: "develop policies that address negative aspects of boy culture, including bullying, name-calling and sexual harassment"; "analyze [curriculum] resources for gender bias"; "use the promise of success when questioning boys"; "challenge stereotypes and help develop a caring masculinity"; "encourage boys' involvement in expressive arts"; "give boys more responsibility around the school"; "provide counseling on the same basis, including peer counseling"; "give pupils pastoral support roles" (Wilson, 2003, pp. 37–39).

Personal, Social and Health Education also plays a key role in Wilson's suggestions, which include dealing explicitly with gender issues such as including peer pressure and sexual harassment, focusing on personal behavior as well as developing personal skills such as cooperation and negotiation, encouraging boys to play a more active role in aspects of school organization and in work in the local community, promoting cooperation as the key to success, ensuring equal access to all sports, and establishing a pupils' sports council. A useful strategy recommended was linking upper school pupils to Year 7 [lower] forms in a pastoral support role that can have benefits for both groups.

The Healthy School approach is echoed to some extent in the "productive pedagogies" model advocated by Mills and Keddie (2005). This model, while having the capacity to provide "a high quality education for *all* students" can also cater to "the specifics of boys' education" through a "focus on teaching boys about notions of social/gender justice, and the responsibilities such notions imply for living in a democratic society" (Mills & Keddie, 2005, p. 4). The productive pedagogies framework highlights the value of the teacher's ability to prioritize relationships with students, and cites Darling-Hammond (1997: 134), who states that "relationships matter for learning," and Lingard, Martino, Mills, & Bahr (2002) as proponents of building relationships with students. Support in the classroom, according to Mills and Keddie, based on work done by the *Queensland School Reform Longitudinal Study* (QSRLS), involves students being given a voice in the classroom with a view to determining the types of activities used in classes. They support their view with that of Hargreaves (2003: 47), who has noted that "care must be more than charity or control: it must become a relationship in which those who are cared for have agency, dignity and a voice." Mills and Keddie (2005) suggest that we must be concerned about authoritarian structures in some schools that stifle dissent and focus more on democratic disciplinary approaches that share power and authority as the modus operandi. They also argue that schools must teach boys especially how to communicate effectively since this is instrumental in developing and maintaining relationships, and teach them explicitly about gender while taking care not to "undo" the effort by perpetuating traditional stances on expectations of masculinity. In addition, they suggest that teaching boys how to value differences in people can stem the problematic wave created by dominant constructions of masculinity with their attendant oppressive behaviors. An important part of the productive pedagogies is the facilitation of a "pedagogy of emotions" which would "encourage the development of boys' capacities for expressing their own feelings and for expressing sympathy and emotional connectedness with others" (Mills & Keddie, 2005, p. 11). Ensuring that curricula are based on real world issues and that students' work is sufficiently intellectually challenging are other salient factors proposed by Mills and Keddie (2005) in their argument for changing classrooms "in ways that promote social justice as an ideal for boys" (p. 18).

In Trinidad and Tobago, the issue of teacher gender balance has surfaced. In a newspaper article (2010), it was reported that first vice president of the Trinidad and Tobago Unified Teachers Association (TTUTA) said that salary negotiations with the government were being done with the aim of attracting more male teachers to the profession. He commented that "the short supply of men in the teaching profession has serious learning implication outcomes in students because of the gender imbalance, particularly in the secondary system and to a lesser extent in the primary." He noted that "traditionally men have dominated in the teaching of mathematics, sciences and technical vocational subjects...

[and that] many teachers in these subjects use teaching only as a stepping stone" (*The Guardian*, Sep. 2010).

The school under study is an all boys secondary school which is church affiliated but receives most of its funding from the government. Until recent years it has had a long tradition of male administrative leadership and a predominantly male teaching staff. It has a record of high achievement and is associated with high academic achievement and notable participation in cricket and football.

Traditionally seen as a "prestige school" with expectations of high achievement, its broader social setting is one that sees young males underperforming generally. However, this school, because of the local education system, receives students from among the highest performers in a national entrance examination. Academic achievement is generally satisfactory and beyond. A small team of experienced teachers in the school have expressed their concern that the students do not seem to be developing the kinds of attitudes and behaviors which they deem appropriate for young males in that society. Their concern was also that the number of male teachers has diminished over the years with only about one-third of the staff being male, whereas in former years, the situation was the opposite. They felt that it was an issue that warranted further research. Thus, a research plan was designed and implemented.

Methodology

A descriptive case study approach was employed in this research which is a single case featuring both qualitative and quantitative methodologies. It focuses on the contemporary phenomenon of school culture within its real-life context. Boundaries between the phenomenon and its context are not clear due to the nature of adolescent development and the many psycho-social factors that impact it.

The questions this research sought to answer are:

1 What are student's perceptions of the importance of certain qualities to their self-development?
2 What are student's perceptions of the importance of certain skills to their self-development?
3 How do students perceive the school's input in their personal development?

4. What are students' perceptions of teacher input into their personal development?
5. What are students' suggestions/recommendations for better input by teachers and school into their overall development?
6. What are teachers' views on the need for male teacher input in the development of students at the school?

An interview with a three-member team of teachers from the school identified a concern about the inadequate level of male input into the students' holistic development, with an emphasis on personal development. Discussion resulted in the need to ascertain the views of students and teachers with regard to students' needs in terms of their holistic development, but more so in terms of their personal development.

A focus group interview with eight random students from Forms Three to Six generated feedback about their needs as male students. A semi-structured guide was used to conduct this interview. The content of the interview was used to develop a questionnaire for the target group of 100 students in all. Forty-one students completed questionnaires within school time anonymously.

Two focus group interviews with teachers provided data on teachers' views on the issue.

Findings

Students' ranking of qualities

This section of the data analysis concerns students' perceptions of the importance of certain qualities to their self-development. The section is subdivided according to the sub-headings that follow.

Overall ranking of qualities

Figure 6.1 represents students' rating of how important certain qualities are to their self-development. They rated the qualities on a scale of 1–5 with 1 being the lowest.

High ranking qualities

Figure 6.1 shows that larger numbers of students felt that *tolerance* and *discipline* were very important to their self-development—in each case 22

Should We Re-Masculinize the Boys School? 131

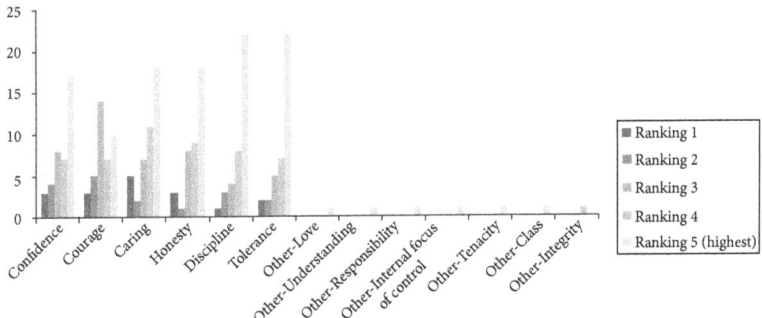

FIGURE 6.1 *Students' ranking of the importance of certain qualities to their self-development*

out of 41. *Honesty* was ranked as very important by 18 out of 41 students and *confidence* was very important to 17 out of 41.

If we were to combine categories 4 and 5 representing the two highest rankings in the 5-point scale, we would note that *discipline* ranked high in importance for 30 out of 41 of the students, with *tolerance* being important to almost as many of them. *Honesty* was ranked as important by the 3rd highest number of students followed by *caring* and *confidence* by almost the same number of students. Generally, more than half of the respondents found discipline, tolerance, honesty, caring and confidence to be important to their self-development. Although less than a half of the students (16) found *courage* to be of high importance, another 14 ranked it as "3" on the scale (as seen in Figure 6.1), indicating that it was of some importance to them in terms of their self-development.

Although each of the following qualities was introduced in each instance as important to one student, they are worthy of mention in order to highlight what educators may overlook in their approach to students' overall development: love, understanding, responsibility, internal focus of control, tenacity, class, integrity. In the focus interview, students mentioned additionally optimism, punctuality and respect for others as qualities they considered important to their holistic development. Following is a summary quoting the elements required for holistic development from the perspective of teachers, gleaned from the focus group interview with them:

▸ communication skills including listening;

- lack of "nerdiness";
- strong sense of integrity which represents the values of [name of school];
- (being) imaginative, creative;
- social responsibility;
- gentlemanly conduct;
- good moral values;
- courtesy/etiquette;
- respect for elders;
- leadership skills;
- sense of purpose;
- strong sense of identity—personal and social.

Low ranking qualities

Although higher proportions of students ranked all six qualities (confidence, caring, honesty, discipline and tolerance) as important or very important, it is significant that there were quite a few students who did not perceive these qualities to be important to their self-development.

Of those students indicating a low interest in the six qualities, most show little interest in *courage*. The number who valued *confidence* and *caring* was a little lower, while still fewer had little interest in *honesty, discipline* and *tolerance*.

Student ranking of the six qualities was as follows in descending order:

- discipline;
- tolerance;
- honesty;
- caring;
- confidence;
- courage.

Personal skills that students consider important to their self-development

This section outlines the students' ranking of certain personal skills in terms of importance to their self-development.

Time management, getting along with others, and *handling conflict* were the personal skills rated the highest by the largest number of students. *Assessing my needs* was important to almost as many as the three skills indicated before, and *expressing my opinions, expressing my feelings,* and *teamwork* were also ranked as important but not by as many students as the four other skills.

High ranking personal skills

Handling conflict, time management, and *getting along with others* were significantly important to the largest number of students, ranging from 23 to 26 out of 41. Yet, in each instance, six students rated these three skills as being of low importance to their self-development. Around 18 to 19 students felt that *expressing their opinion, assessing their needs,* and *teamwork* were significantly important to their self-development whereas four to eight students found these skills to be low in importance. *Expressing their feelings* was ranked as important by only 14 of the students and a relatively high number of them (10) found this skill to be of low importance.

Students' opinion of school's contribution to their personal development

Developing Qualities

There was a general trend that more students felt that the school was preparing them at least to some extent in terms of qualities necessary to their personal development. The smallest number of students felt that *courage* and *caring* were the qualities that received least attention in school from these students' perspective. The largest numbers of students felt that the school was preparing them to be *disciplined* (17/41), *honest* (15/41) and *tolerant* (14/41) to a large extent. More than half of the students felt that there was a fairly good to very good effort by the school to prepare them for all six qualities. Even with the combined numbers for "to a great extent" and "to some extent", *courage* and *caring* ranked relatively lowest in terms of the number of students who felt that the school was preparing them to develop these qualities.

Little or no effort by school

A noteworthy number of students felt that the school was not contributing significantly to their personal development. Those numbers ranged from 6 to as high as 14. Once more, *courage* and *caring* are areas that a significant number of students felt were hardly or not attended to at school. There were isolated single cases who shared the view that the school prepared them in terms of religion (2 students) and understanding (1 student) to a great extent, dealing with girls (1 student) and "fight control" (1 student) to some extent, moral judgment (1 student) and integrity (1 student) hardly, and responsibility (1 student) not at all. Even though these are isolated cases, small numbers of students who are disillusioned or who feel inadequately prepared in terms of their personal development provide sufficient justification for propelling policy-makers towards greater efforts at human development and fulfilling our purpose of "education for all".

Developing personal skills

Overall, larger numbers of students felt that the school was attending to developing personal skills "to some extent" as opposed "to a large extent". This was the case for five out of the seven skills: *teamwork, getting along with others, expressing my feelings, expressing my opinions* and *handling conflict*. The same number of students (12) felt that they were learning to *assess their needs* to a "large extent" and "to some extent".

When "to a large extent" and "to some extent" were combined, more than half of the students felt that the school was providing input at least to some extent in addressing all seven of these skills for their personal development. Even though more than half of the student respondents felt that all these skills were being addressed at least to some extent, it is useful to note that significant numbers felt that they were either hardly being addressed or not at all. Those numbers ranged between 8 and 17, which, for a total of 41 students, is a significant proportion (20%–41%).

One student expressed the view that the school attended to *respecting others* to a great extent. If one compares how students rated the various qualities that impact their personal development with to what extent the school provides for the nurturing of these qualities, we would see that for every quality, the number of students who felt that the school provided opportunity for its development was larger than the number who felt that the actual quality was significantly important. This may indicate that students do not always appreciate the value of personal lessons taught at the school. The largest discrepancy is seen in the areas of *courage* and *confidence*. More than half of the students seem to recognize that the school places value on these, but significantly fewer deem these two qualities as important to their personal development.

When one compares how students rated the various skills that contribute to their personal development with to what extent the school provides for the nurturing of these skills, the findings showed that except for *handling conflict*, which showed consistency in students' rating of its importance and the extent of the school's provision for its development, the number of students indicating that the school provided for the development of the other skills was always higher than the number of students who thought that the skills were important to some or to a large extent.

In the focus interview, the students agreed that the school should "show you what to do, guide you" in terms of their personal development. Citing punctuality as an example, they felt that the school could teach students to be punctual by "putting penalties if deadlines weren't met." They did agree that if an assignment affected a grade they would treat it with more urgency meaning that their inclination to be punctual depended on the importance they attached to the task. Academic achievement was high as a priority.

In the interview one student expressed the view that there was too much emphasis on only three sports at the school: volleyball, cricket, and football. He felt that these "were put on a pedestal" and that the "others were hung out to dry." Another wanted "equal opportunity to show their skills" and to participate in sports, and felt that a variety should be offered for recreational purposes rather than competition. They would like sports to be included in the regular curriculum: "Because [name of school] stresses on holistic development shouldn't it be in the curriculum?" They deplored the poor sporting facilities which discourage participation. They also felt that more opportunity to learn Music, PE, and Art should be provided within the main curriculum in Forms Four and Five, but not necessarily as academic subjects but as a stress reliever. There was mention of overemphasis on the steelpan as a musical instrument when there could be more opportunity for playing the piano or other instruments. Even though there is a music club, the main instrument is the guitar and these are brought by the students themselves. One of their concerns about forming a choir was the stigma attached to it from a male perspective. They admitted that they are sometimes unable to oppose the idea that "male society wants this tough guy image."

Time was cited as one of their major obstacles to participating in activities which would help them to develop personal skills. "Teachers overwork us with projects." Even when there is group work with projects "group work is a challenge" "because sometimes in a group some people slack off and you pull all their weight and I don't like that." Although they do try to "do fun stuff," after a while "parents begin to crunch down on fun because of projects... exams... study."

Teachers' views on actual student development

All 10 teachers interviewed agreed that they've sensed a lack of male influence in their students' school life. As to why students were not developing as fully as they would like them to in terms of their personal development, teachers' responses varied. One teacher indicated that there was insufficient attention to drama as a curricular offering and there was a vacancy for a drama teacher at the school. Also, while there existed a number of clubs and societies at the school, these were not a high priority for students. Instead "they just sit around and do nothing; they don't want to do anything constructive." One teacher recommended that credits be given for participating in clubs. They agreed that parents do not see extra-curricular activities as important and that "students are heavily influenced by parents."

Students' perceptions of which teachers helped them to develop the qualities and skills

Figure 6.2 reveals how students recognized which teachers help them with the development of the skills and qualities necessary for their personal growth. What stands out is that most of them felt that male teachers helped them to develop discipline, which was a quality rated by the largest number of students as important to their personal development.

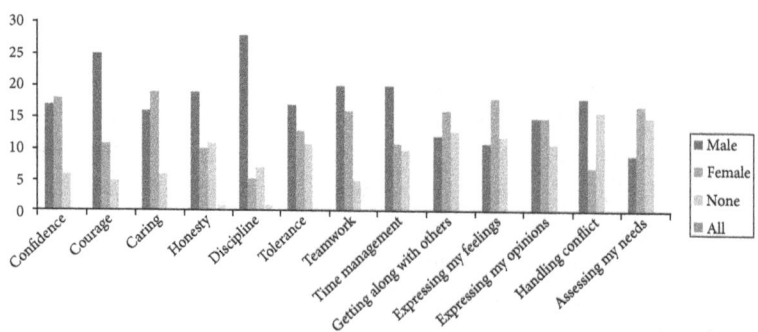

FIGURE 6.2 *Number of students indicating which teachers helped to develop their qualities and skills*

This response to their male teachers is in keeping with some students' perception noted later in this analysis that male teachers are required to establish discipline in male students.

Even though there are more female teachers than male on the staff at this school, more students selected male teachers as the ones who have helped them to develop teamwork and tolerance, and a significantly larger number of students selected male teachers over female teachers as the ones who helped them to develop time management, honesty, courage, and handling conflict. It must be noted that in many instances a single teacher had an impact on students in more than one quality or skill.

Females were selected more often than males for 4 out of 13 "development essentials". More students named female teachers over male teachers as the ones who developed their ability to get along with others and to express their feelings and for developing their caring and the ability to assess their needs.

Students' responses indicated that the ability to express their opinion was nurtured equally by male and female teachers, and their confidence level was developed almost equally by male and by female teachers.

While most students were able to indicate which teachers were instrumental in helping with some aspect of their personal development, for every quality or skill there were some students who did not select any teacher. These numbers ranged from 5 to 16. Sixteen students did not select teachers who helped them to handle conflict and 15 did not select any who enabled them to assess their needs. Apart from those, more than 10 students did not name any teacher who helped them to be honest, to be tolerant, to get along with others, to express their feelings, or to express their opinion. Out of a total of 41 students, these numbers are significant.

While almost all the students were able to identify teachers for most or all of the items, two of them selected teachers for only two of the items, and one student did not select any teacher for any item. It is not possible to determine why from these data.

Between 10 and 16 students did not select teachers for the following items: time-management (10), expressing my opinion (11), expressing my feelings (12), getting along with others (13), assessing my needs (15), and handling conflict (16). These are six of the seven skills deemed by this discussion to be essential to personal development. Essentially, almost one-quarter to more than one-half of the sample did not feel that these needs were being met by their teachers.

What is perplexing is that of the 16 students who indicated that there was no male figure at school whom they looked up to, with the exception of one student, all of them had selected at least one male teacher who had helped with their personal development in some way.

A male figure to look up to at school

Twenty-two out of the 41 students said that there was a male figure at school whom they looked up to. Sixteen said there were none. Three gave no response.

In the focus interview there was consensus that there was no male figure at school that they looked up to. It may mean that the impact of the help that had received was not sufficient to warrant "looking up to" the teacher. The interview responses introduced one student's concept of a role model: "a role model...you want to be like them, but respecting them is different from wanting to be like them." It may also point to the possibility that what a student learns from a teacher has no bearing on how the student perceives the teacher in terms of "look up to"—perhaps that term was open to a variety of interpretations. In this context its intended meaning was "respect", "emulate", "be inspired by", "have a high regard for". In describing the qualities of a role model one student said, "strict but not severe, understanding, won't punish you for the smallest thing...but not a pushover...a nice balance."

The following are verbatim reasons which the students cited for looking up to a male figure at their school:

- fair and understanding; understands;
- straight forward;
- good role model;
- cares for the students;
- friendly and interacts with students; able to relate to students;
- teaches you to be a man;
- good teacher; a brilliant teacher;
- well disciplined;
- inspirational and successful and I aspire to follow in his footsteps;
- grasps students' attention;
- smart;
- leader of the school;
- teaches good moral values;
- accomplishments and approach to everyday activities;

- taught me discipline and motivated me to pursue dreams greater than I imagined;
- has inspired me to grasp every opportunity and make the best of it;
- has taught me discipline, tolerance, and production;
- a respected person who works hard to help others;
- displays many qualities that I admire;
- taught me many life lessons.

Current situation of "more female teachers"— does it matter to students?

There are currently more female teachers than male at the all boys school. Students were asked to respond to this specific situation of the presence of more female than male teachers which was of concern to some teachers. Fifteen students indicated that this issue mattered to them. Some supported the predominance of female teachers (positive reasons) while some did not (negative reasons). Not all students gave reasons.

The positive reasons given were that the school was "already dominated by boys"; "females are more helpful"; "more caring than males"; "we need to know how to interact with the opposite sex"; "I love the way they teach"; "seeing the opposite sex on a daily basis keeps a good balance in my life."

The negative reasons for students' concern were that "the students get distracted"; "if disagreements and violence they [female teachers] have no hold over them [the students]"; "females cannot control a set of teenagers full of raging hormones"; "topics of a male student which female teachers cannot relate to and resolve"; "some females carry themselves in a degrading manner which causes male distraction"; "female teachers cannot control all-male class"; "men are able to explain topics easier and relate to students".

In the interview students recalled their male teacher in the lower Form who was "very, very strict, but you understood what he was saying"..."you sort of looked up to him". Another was "strict also but he did make us understand...he made jokes." They typify their female teachers as "not very harsh" and "more understanding." These students do not miss the male input at school. One view was the "females are getting the job done, maybe even better." They felt it "was easier to ask questions" with the female teachers without the fear of being humiliated. They didn't see the need to employ more male teachers and felt they were better suited to being deans. One student believed that "fear breeds respect." This indicates that students' understanding of respect may vary.

Twenty-five students said that it did not matter to them that there were more female teachers than male. Some students did not give reasons. The following are the verbatim reasons given:

- Already a lot of male students and male teachers.
- No, because I come here to learn.
- Education is all that matters.
- I get educated either way.
- Does not affect my opinion of the teacher.
- I feel comfortable since I have a mother as a single parent.
- If individual has self-discipline presence of male figure is not necessary.
- As long as there are no problems with how they interact with the students.
- As long that there are enough male teachers to maintain harmony.
- I guess not, they are like my mothers away from home.
- I do most of the work on my own anyway.

One student was neutral on the issue which he found "insignificant depending on your perspective on female teachers' role."

Ways in which male teachers can help more with students' personal development

All but one student offered suggestions as to how male teachers could help more with their personal development. Eight of them suggested talking with students about "male" things and more informal interaction: "interact with me about manly things & my development as a male"; "take time to talk to the students as a fatherly role"; "identifying with students and conversing with them on an informal level." Ten of them felt that teachers could use their own experiences for students to draw from to arrive at some common understandings: "all of them went through what we are going through and they can relate to us"; "they have experienced what we have before and can give advice"; "motivation through personal experiences"; "they would be better able to deal with certain situations having had past experience of their own."

Six students offered suggestions about giving advice and being exemplars: "about being more disciplined and growing into a gentleman in the outside world"; "they act as role models"; "counseling and assisting with matters which burden students"; "teach us personal tips about life." Other suggestions were "implementing sports"; "make clubs and organize activities and meetings"; "help in time management"; "teaching us how to communicate with each other"; "they can help you to have integrity"; "they should be a little less rough and more helpful and understanding"; "be better role models."

Five students did not feel that the male teachers could be of any more help with their personal development.

One male teacher identified some qualities which he felt constituted his role as a male teacher in the school. He suggested honesty, responsibility, independence, leadership, gentlemanly conduct, how to make allowances, how to forgive. Another male teacher stated that "regardless of the subject you teach, students look to you as a pattern." While there was the view that "students are impressed by female teachers because they're motherly and friendly," a related comment was that "the male teachers are the ones who have the most impact." In consideration of the latter comment, one female teacher observed that "a lot of the male teachers are not involved in extra-curricular, except as coach or sports coordinator, but not in clubs that involve talking, discussing." Another comment was that "more male teachers should be more vocal and visible, for example in morning assembly. Only about three are. Others need to step up." One teacher observed that the older students seem to be more open with male teachers about sensitive issues such as human sexuality, whilst the younger ones seem to respond more easily to female teachers. Interestingly, one male teacher stated that "not all male teachers share the same philosophy with regard to what we want of students," and this comment was immediately qualified by another teacher who said "not all *male* teachers but *all* teachers." By the time the discussion was closing, the general feeling was that it was not so much a "male vs. female" issue but a "culture" issue. The comment was made that due to high staff turnover the culture of the school was being threatened as teachers no longer have a unified culture as in the past. Five of the ten teachers interviewed still felt that there was a need for more male teachers.

Students' recommendations to school

Students were asked to suggest ways in which the school can help them more with their personal development. There were four themes which students commented on most.

Teachers

Seven students made comments relating to teachers. Among four of them there was the opinion that the school should get rid of a total of five named teachers. Another felt that teachers needed to develop more "in terms of communication, interaction and knowledge of syllabus requirements." One student's view was that "teachers need to be more understanding and caring especially Mr. _____ who curses students." Another view was that teachers "interacting with students on a personal level" would be helpful. "One on One talks" was a suggestion made by another student.

From the comments above, it would seem that more of the "softer" side of pedagogy is what students may appreciate, in addition to "syllabus requirements." *Caring* was important to a significantly high number of students but 14 students felt that *caring* was hardly or not addressed in school as a quality they need for their personal development.

It is interesting that one student expressed the view that "being tolerant to students expressing their honest opinions" was something that teachers could do to help them develop on a personal level. This echoes the finding above that although 28 out of 41 students felt that the school helped to build their ability to express their opinions, 13 out of 41 felt that there was hardly any or no effort at this at the school level. There are clearly conflicting views which would depend on the varying interactions of different students.

Activities

Five students made comments related to the idea that activities could help with their personal development. One student suggested that the school "implement activities that challenge the students' confidence, caring, honesty, discipline," while another recommended "compulsory activities for personal development." Three students were more specific, suggesting "more sports to become more social"; "more Active Clubs with no discrimination"; and "Debate club."

It is evident that these students see a positive relationship between participation in activities and the development of qualities and skills that would enable personal growth.

Girls

Five students offered suggestions that indicate their need to socialize with girls. Two of the related comments were that "girls should be allowed to open up guys into developing emotions so they can relate to them" and that the school should "bring girls into the school so we can interact with them in many ways."

Human support

Four students mentioned the need for a structured human support system. Two suggested a system of guidance counseling and one recommended "the opportunity to interact with peer 'councilors' [sic] and teachers to express feelings." A third recommendation was a "big brother program."

Other

Three students felt they needed help with time management. Two others felt that the school should not have any female students. Another two recommended better school facilities. Other recommendations that were made were:

- more confidence in preparing for exams;
- extra lessons;
- developing better holistic approach to school life.

Two students felt that it is up to the student to develop personally rather than the school facilitating it and three of them felt that there was nothing the school could do.

Students' recommendations to principal regarding "male vs. female teachers" with reasons

Teachers should be male

Students' responses to the above statement: Yes: 19; No: 18; Neutral: 2.

Nineteen students were of the opinion that the principal should employ more male teachers. Ten of them cited either discipline or control as their reason. For example, one said that "male teachers have a stronger hold over students" and another said that "a dominant male figure is needed to keep control." Other comments included "they are more strict," "they command respect better." Eight students felt that because the school is an all boys school, male teachers are better suited, and some specified that this was because students need role models or teachers who would better understand them: "males need role models they can emulate and who can relate to them in specific needs and challenges"; "male teachers would understand us more."

Three students expressed the view that female teachers are a distraction, thus a preference for male teachers, while two commented that some of their female teachers dressed inappropriately. One such comment was: "some female teachers dress in a disgusting manner with no self-respect."

No more male teachers needed

Eighteen students were of the view that the principal should *not* employ more male teachers. Eight students felt this way because there are already too many male teachers. Two indicated that the idea of the opposite sex was appealing to them: "I'm attracted to the opposite sex"; "It is a boy school and I like girls." One felt that the female input was important because of boys' developmental needs and a need for a female perspective. One student commented that males don't teach well.

For two students it did not matter whether teachers were male or female.

Teachers' recommendations

The following recommendations were made by individual teachers in the focus group interview.

Implicit in the complaint that not enough male teachers are involved in clubs other than sports is the suggestion that more male teachers should be accessible to students outside of class time for informal talks and interaction. This was especially important as some teachers prefer not to deal with topics outside of the curriculum in class time.

There was also the recommendation that students needed to have a sense of purpose, to understand why they were learning what they were learning in school. In addition, school must make the effort to ensure that students must be able to pass on their positive values and traditions to their own children.

Due to the perception of a threatened school culture, it was suggested that orientation for new students should take place earlier than it does now, and that it be a formal set program that should not depend solely on Form teachers since some of them may be relatively new to the school. The issue of fast staff turnover also prompted the recommendation that mentorship be instituted to maintain the desired culture of the school.

Discussion and conclusion

When one considers the purpose of schooling to be to educate the learner in the truest sense of the word, the role of personal development becomes evident. Generally the students at this school, in varying degrees, recognize the value of developing qualities such as discipline, tolerance, honesty, caring, confidence, and courage, and skills such as handling conflict, time management, getting along with others, expressing opinions, assessing one's needs, teamwork, and expressing one's feelings in order to enhance their personal growth.

There is evidence from the students' feedback that, to some extent, the school provides for the development of relevant qualities and skills, even though some students do not value these as much as the school does if one judges by the school's provision as perceived by some of the students.

When one examines the suggestions made by students, what stands out is the human element which many of them desire from their male teachers, with an emphasis on teacher-student communication and relationships. This is reflected in the teacher's suggestion that male teachers should be accessible to students outside of class time for informal talks and interaction. The suggested teacher-teacher mentorship appears to be an appropriate avenue for developing and increasing the positive male teacher behaviors identified by some students.

The question remains, though, whether we should be developing "male" adolescents or simply "adolescents" (Rowe and Rowe, 2002; Mills et al., 2004). While we must heed the caution against the "hegemonic masculinity" discussed by Martino and Frank (2006), we must also acknowledge Wilson's conception of the "Healthy School," which seeks to develop the best in the male student. Depending on one's concept of the role model, and if one agrees that there is some inherent difference between male and female persons, then one has no alternative but to make provision for the balanced development of males in an all male school. This study brings to bear students' voices on this matter within this specific context.

References

Biddulph, S. (1995). *Manhood: An Action Plan for Changing Men's Lives* (2nd edn). Sydney: Finch.

Burn, E. (2001). "Do boys need male primary teachers as positive role models?" Paper presented to the British Educational Research Association Annual Conference, University of Leeds, September 13–15, 2001.

Kindler, D. & Thompson, M. (1999). *Raising Cain: Protecting the Emotional Life of Boys*. London, Michael Joseph.

Lingard, B., Martino, W., Mills, M., & Bahr, M. (2002). *Addressing the Educational Needs of Boys*. Canberra, ACT, Australia: Department of Education, Science and Training. Retrieved September 30, 2009, from HYPERLINK "http://www.deewr.gov.au/schooling/BoysEducation/pages/default.aspx" www.deewr.gov.au/schooling/BoysEducation/pages/default.aspx.

Martin, A. (2002). *Improving the Educational Outcomes of Boys*. Report to ACT Department of Education, Youth and Family Services, Canberra: AAACT Government.

Martino, W. & Frank, B. (2006). The tyranny of surveillance: male teachers and the policing of masculinities in a single sex school. *Gender and Education. 18*, 1, January, 17–33.

Martino, W. & Kehler, M. (2006). Male teachers and the "boy problem": an issue of recuperative masculinity politics, *McGill Journal of Education, 41*, 2, Spring.

Martino, W. & Meyenn, B. (eds.) (2001). *What about the boys? Issues of masculinity and schooling,* Buckingham: Open University Press.

Mills, M., & Keddie, A. (2005). "Boys, Productive Pedagogies and Social Justice". Paper presented at the AARE Conference, University of Western Sydney, University of Sydney, November–December 2005.

Mills, M., Martino, W. & Lingard, B. (2004). Attracting, recruiting and retaining male teachers: policy issues in the male teachers debate, *British Journal of the Sociology of Education, 25,* 3, 355–369.

Pollack, W. (1999). *Real Boys: Rescuing Our Sons from the Myths of Boyhood*. New York. Henry Holt.

Rowe, K. & Rowe, K. (2002). *What matters most: evidence-based findings of key factors affecting the educational experiences and outcomes for girls and boys throughout their primary and secondary schooling.* Supplementary submission to Australian House of Representative Standing Committee on Education and Training: *Inquiry into the Education of Boys*. May.

Skelton, C. (2003). Male primary teachers and perceptions of masculinity, *Educational Review, 55,* 2, 195–209.

Smedley, S. (1998). Perspectives on male primary teachers *Changing English, 5,* 147–159.

Smith, S. (2004). *Teaching and the Gender Imbalance: Do We Need More MATES?* Central Queensland University.

Wilson, G. (2003). *Use the National Healthy School Standard to Raise Boys' Achievement*. London: Department for Education.

Index

Abele, A. E., 100
academic achievement, 135
academic advice, 105
action research, 3
adolescent stress, 58
"agency," 85
Ainley, J., Robinson, L., Harvey-Beavis, A., Elsworth, G., & Fleming, M., 121
Akey, T. M, 100
all-rounded education, 37
Altrichter, H., Posch, P., & Somekh, B., 24
Ames, C., 100
anxiety, 59, 62, 100, 126
Apple Learning Exchange, 31
Arnett, Jeffrey Jensen, 80
Arnett, Jensen Jeffrey, 80
Arun, Priti & Chavan, B. S., 80
assumptions and beliefs, 29

Bandura, A., 100, 102
Benton, S. A., Robertson, J. M., Tseng, W., Newton, F. B., & Benton, S. L., 80
Berger, R., 54
Bernhardt, V., 25
Bevan, R. M., 25
Biddulph, S., 145
Brunner, R., Parzer, P., Haffner, J., Steen, R., Roos, J., Klett, M., & Resch, F., 81
Burn, E., 145

Butt, R., Raymond, D., McCue, G., & Yamagishi, L., 25
"buy in," 15, 19

career choice, 104
Career Day, 118
career decisions, 104
    occupational interest, 104
Care, E. & Naylor, F., 121
career guidance, 105, 106, 116
career path, 110, 111, 113
career programme, 106
career development, 106
caring, 132, 142
caring teacher, 87
Chapman, R., 121
character education, 33
Character Education Partnership, 31, 54
Chen, E., Heritage, M., & Lee, J., 25
Choppin, J., 25
Clandinin, D., & Connelly, M., 25
Cobain, B., 81
Coburn, C., Honig, M. I., & Stein, M. K., 25
cognitive social theory, 85
Cohen, L., Manion, L., & Morrison, K., 121
collaborative work, 13
Colten, E. M. & Gore, S., 81
competent system, 6, 23

competition, 17, 29, 30, 57, 58, 63, 87, 90, 95, 135
complexity theory, 34
Conor, P. E. & Lake, L. K., 54
contagion theory, 86, 100
coping with stress, 57, 60
courtesy and politeness, 39, 41
"crisis of masculinity," 125
culture of collaboration, 7, 23
curriculum planning, 98

Darling-Hammond, L., & Ascher, C., 25
data-driven decision-making, 3
Deal, T. E., 54
dealing with Stress, 71
De Charms, R., 54
Deci, E. L., & Ryan, R. M., 100
De Lisle, J., Seecharan, H., & Ayodike, A. T., 25
Dellar, G., 121
denominational schools, 2
depression, 59, 62
diligence, 40
disappointments, 94, 99
discipline, 136
disillusion, 30, 117
dissatisfactions, 98
"doing school," 62

Eccles, J. S., & Midgley, C., 101
Eccles, J. S., Midgley, C., Wigfield, A., Buchanan, M., Reuman, D., Flanagan, C., & Mac Iver, D., 101
Edwards, K. & Quinter, M., 121
Einstein, D. A., Lovibond, P. F. & Gaston, J. E., 81
Elbot, C.F. & Fulton, D., 54
enthusiasm, 10
ethos, 52
examination grades, 99
excellence, 45, 50
experiences of school, 93

Fadell L. W. & Tempkow, S. E., 101
failing boys, 126
Feldman, J. & Tung, R., 25

female teachers, 124, 126, 137, 139, 140, 141, 143, 144
Finnan, C., 54
"fit in," 29
Fong, K. I. S., 54
"forced choices," 109, 115
formal research, 11

gaining entry, 9
"get ahead," 58
Gibson, L., 81
goal identification, 105, 120
goal of schooling, 124
Goldberg, M. F., 101
Goodson, I. F., & Hargreaves, A., 26
Gordon, S.P., 26
Guar, C. B., Murthy, A. & Nathawat, S. S., 81
Gullekson, D., 121
Gutman, L. M. & Eccles, J. S., 101

Hall, G. S., 81
Handscomb, G., & MacBeath, J., 26
Hardré, P. L., 101
Hardré, P. L., & Reeve, J., 101
Hardré, P. L., & Sullivan, D. W., 101
Hardy, L., 54, 81
Hargreaves, D., 26
Harvey, M. J., 121
Hayes, S. C., Wilson, K. G., Gifford, E.V., Follette, V.M. & Strosahl, K. D., 81
healthy school standard, 127
Heaven, P.C.L. & Ciarrochi, J., 101
"hidden curriculum," 53
Higgins, E. T., 81
Higgins, E. T., & Kruglanski, A., 101
Higgins, E. T., & Parsons, J. E., 102
high achievers, 62
high expectations, 31, 32, 43, 44, 58, 60, 86, 87, 94
high ranking qualities, 130
high standards, 58
Hinde, E. R., 55
Hodkinson, P. & Sparkes, A. C., 121
Holcomb, E.L., 26

holistic development, 35, 46, 47, 79, 96, 123, 125, 130, 131, 135
home-related stress, 69
homework, 79
Hoyle, E., 55
human element, 145

informal interaction, 140
informal research, 12
Ingram, D., Seashore Louis, K., & Schroeder, R. D., 26
input data, 5
insider, 8, 107, *See also* insiderness
"insiderness," 8

Kai-Wen, C., 81
Kiefer, S. M. & Ryan, A. M., 102
Kilpatrick, W., 55
Kindler, D. & Thompson, M., 145
Kohn, A., 55
Kumar, R., O'Malley, P. M., & Johnston, P. D., 102

Lachat, M.A., & Smith, S., 26
lack of time, 10
Lalwani, S., Sharma, G.A., Kabra, S. K., Girdhar, S. & Dogra, T.D., 81
Lashway, L., 26
Latha, K.S. & Reddy, H., 81
Leithwood, K., Leonard, L. & Sharratt, L., 55
Lickona, L. Schaps, E., & Lewis, C., 55
life goals, 84, 85
life-skills, 61
Lingard, B., Martino, W., Mills, M., & Bahr, M., 146
Little Flower, A., Vazir, S., Fernandez Rao, S., Rao, V., Laxmaiah, A.& Nair, K. M., 81
Locke, E.A., & Latham, G.P., 102
Lockwood, A. L., 55
Logaraj, M., Felix, J.W., & Vedapriya, D. R., 82
Love, N., 26

low academic performance, 84, 96
low motivation, 84
Lumby, J. & Foskett, N., 55

macro policy, 5
male identity, 124
male hegemonic identity, 124
male role models, 124
Mandinach, E., Honey, M., Light, D., & Brunner, C., 26
Mansfield, C. F. & Wosnitza, M., 102
March, J. A., Pane, J. F., & Hamilton. L. S., 26
Martin, A., 146
Martinez-Pons, M., 102
Martino, W. & Frank, B., 146
Martino, W. & Kehler, M., 146
Martino, W. & Meyenn, B., 146
masculinity, 126
hegemonic masculinity, 126
heterosexualized masculinity, 126
Mason, S., 27
micro policy, 5
Mieles, T. & Foley, E., 27
Mills, M. & Keddie, A., 146
Mills, M., Martino, W. & Lingard, B., 146
mixed method approach, 8
morals and values, 98
Morrison, K., 121
motivational theories, 84
Muus, R. E., 82

National Foundation for Educational Research (NFER), 2

Ohi, S., 27
outcome data, 5, 22
outsider, 10
Owens, R., 55

Pajares, F., & Urdan, T., 102
parental advice, 112
parental support, 47
parents' behaviour, 76
Parsons, J. E., 102

pedagogy, 142
  softer side of pedagogy, 142
"pedagogy of emotions," 128
peer influence, 86
perception data, 5, 22
perfectionism, 59
perpetuation, 34
personal growth, 88, 136, 142, 145
personal skills, 132
person-environment fit, 86
person-environment misfit, 99
Peterson, K. D., 55
Pintrich, P. R., 102
Pintrich, P. R., & Schunk, D. H., 102
Pitzer, R. L., 82
Pollack, W., 146
Pope, D. C., 82
"prestige schools," 88
principal's behaviour, 45
process data, 5
"productive pedagogies," 127
professional behaviour, 99
professional development, 3, 8, 13, 16, 17, 21, 32
professional learning community, 6
professionalism, 3, 15
Purpel, D. E., 55

qualitative data, 6, 108
quality of schooling, 125
"quality of teaching," 79

Ramya, N. & Parthasarathy, R., 82
RAND, 6, 26
relevance, 17
research capability, 13
research culture, 1, 2, 3, 8, 12, 21, 27
research-engaged school, 2
research engagement, 2, 23
research findings, 4
research methods, 8, 19
research skills, 16
research team, 1, 2, 8, 10, 11, 16, 18, 19, 22, 36, 108
research-informed professional practice, 2

research-policy-praxis nexus, 4, 22
Richardson, A., 122
ritual, 31
Roberts, B., 27
role model, 40
Rowe, K. & Rowe, K., 146
Ryan, A. M., & Patrick, H., 102

Sarason, S., 55
satisfaction data, 5
school climate, 32, 47, 48
school community, 34
school culture, 28, 144
  threatened school culture, 144
school rules, 36, 38, 39, 40, 53
school's expectations, 43
school-based research, 4
school-related stress, 65
self-development, 129, 130, 131, 132, 133
  low-ranking qualities, 130
self-efficacy, 85, 98, 101, 102
sense of efficacy, 86
Sharp, C., Eames, A., Sanders, D., & Tomlinson, K., 27
Shen, J., Cooley, V., Reeves, P., Burt, W., Ryan, L., Rainey, J. M., & Yuan, W., 27
Siann, G., Lightbody, P., Nicholson, S., Tait, L. & Walsh, D., 122
Silins, H., Zarins, S., & Mulford, B., 55
Simmons, R. G., & Blyth, D. A., 102
single-sex schools, 60
Skelton, C., 146
Slaby, A. & Garfinkel, L. F., 82
Smedley, S., 146
Smith, S., 146
social mobility, 29, 57, 90, 104
social norms, 30
somatic complaints, 59
sources of stress, 65
Spira, J.C., Zvlensky, M.J., Eifert, G.H. & Feldner, M.T., 82
sports, 135
Srikata, B. & Kumar, K.V., 82
Stables, A. & Stables, S., 122
staff turnover, 141, 144

stakeholder empowerment, 5
"storm and stress," 58, 80
student aspirations, 86
student capability, 89
student engagement, 87
student frustration, 99
student satisfaction, 109
student stress, 57, 79
student success, 4, 5, 98
students' behavior, 40
students' confidence, 87, 142
students' goals, 111
students' recommendations, 73, 141, 143
subject choice information, 105
subject offerings, 120
subject selection
  subject choice, 11, 24, 103, 104, 105, 107, 108, 109, 110, 115, 116, 117, 118, 120, 121, 122
success, 58, 86, 92
successful person, 92, 97
Supovitz, J. A. & Klein, V., 27
supportive teachers, 87, 99
symbols, 31
system of selection, 117

Tawaiyole, S. P. K., 122
teacher attitudes, 79
teacher development, 15, 79
teacher effectiveness, 88, 99
teacher-as-leader, 5
teacher-as-researcher, 5

teachers' behaviors, 46
teachers' gender, 123, 124
teacher-student
  communication, 145
team work, 22
tension, 11, 19
test/exam results, 12, 22
time, 9
Torsheim, T. & Wold, B., 82
transformational leaders, 6, 23, 24
Tripney, J., Newman, M., Bangpan, M., Niza, C., MacKintosh, M., & Sinclair, J., 122
Truong, H. Q. T., 122

values transmission, 31

Walker, J., 82
Warton, P. M. & Cooney, G. H., 122
Wheatley project, 62
Whiteley, S. & Porter, J., 122
whole school improvement, 17
Wikeley, F. & Stables, A., 122
Willingham, D., 102
Wilson, E., 27
Wilson, G., 146

Yin, R., 55, 82, 102

Zimmerman, B. J., Bandura, A. & Martinez-Pons, M., 85, 102
Zmuda, A., Kuklis, R., & Kline, E., 27

GPSR Compliance
The European Union's (EU) General Product Safety Regulation (GPSR) is a set of rules that requires consumer products to be safe and our obligations to ensure this.

If you have any concerns about our products, you can contact us on

ProductSafety@springernature.com

In case Publisher is established outside the EU, the EU authorized representative is:

Springer Nature Customer Service Center GmbH
Europaplatz 3
69115 Heidelberg, Germany

www.ingramcontent.com/pod-product-compliance
Lightning Source LLC
LaVergne TN
LVHW041205250326
834689LV00002BA/24